Sing Praise

HYMNS *and* SONGS
for REFRESHING WORSHIP

Melody Edition

Sing Praise is published by Hymns Ancient & Modern Ltd
and the Royal School of Church Music,
both registered charities.

Hymns Ancient & Modern Ltd
13-17 Long Lane
London EC1A 9PN

Sing Praise Melody Edition
First published November 2010

© *Compilation,* Hymns Ancient & Modern Ltd and the RSCM

All rights reserved. No part of this publication which is copyright may be
reproduced, stored in a retrieval system, or transmitted, in any form or by
any means, electronic, mechanical, photocopying, CD or tape recording, or
otherwise without the prior permission of Hymns Ancient & Modern Ltd or
the appropriate copyright owner. Full particulars, where available, of copyright
words and music are given beside each item on page throughout the book.

A catalogue record of this book is available from the British Library.

ISBN 978-1-84825-038-3

Hymns Ancient & Modern ® is a registered trademark of Hymns Ancient & Modern Ltd

Music engraving and typesetting:
Andrew Parker, Ferndown, Dorset BH22 8BB United Kingdom
Printed in the UK by CPI William Clowes, Beccles NR34 7TL

CONTENTS

PREFACE

Why another collection of hymns and songs? Don't we have enough to sing already?

Music is a vital element in worship's power to refresh and transform both individuals and communities; singing together helps build up the Body of Christ. Those involved in preparing this new resource for Christian worship believe that churches should always be on the lookout for ways to 'sing a new song to the Lord', while also valuing what is tried and tested. The book represents a partnership between Hymns Ancient & Modern Ltd and the Royal School of Church Music, seeking to enable choirs and congregations to refresh their sung repertoire without having to replace their current hymn book. It seems fitting that *Sing Praise* is being published at a time when celebrations are underway to mark the one hundred and fiftieth anniversary of the first edition of *Hymns Ancient and Modern*.

There may be surprise in some quarters at the evidence that, in the early part of the twenty-first century, hymns continue to be written in conventional forms as well as in more song-like styles. In making our selection, we have had to exclude some fine material by contemporary wordsmiths, since the book had to be of manageable size. The rich tradition of Christian hymnody in the English-speaking world is very much alive and continues to develop, and we are delighted to present here some texts which are as yet little known in Britain, along with recently written hymns which have already become or are fast becoming 'classics'. Many of these texts are paired with well-known tunes, while a few older texts appear with more recent settings. Several strong new tunes have been found to partner imaginative words.

The editors of *Sing Praise* share a passionate commitment to the continuing significance of hymnody in the lives of individual believers and of worshipping communities. Two of us are members of the Executive Committee of the Hymn Society of Great Britain and Ireland. Two are directly involved with planning and leading cathedral worship, while two are directors of music in parish churches. Two are involved at a national level in liturgical education of various kinds, and three of us help to produce the RSCM's quarterly liturgy planner, *Sunday by Sunday*. We come from a variety of backgrounds and have brought to our task a range of different skills and areas of expertise. Our aim has been to produce a resource with liturgical and musical integrity — not that we always found it easy to agree as to whether particular items satisfied these criteria.

As well as trying to identify the best of what has emerged in recent years, we chose to pay particular attention to subject areas poorly served by traditional hymnody or by contemporary song repertoire. Among these are environmental concern and certain aspects of the Church's mission, as expressed in recent thinking and writing. Anglican clergy make a promise, each time they take up a new post, to 'proclaim the Gospel afresh in each generation'. This task is shared by the whole people of God, whatever their church background, and congregational song has a part to play in this proclamation, while also energizing worshippers to live out the Gospel message in the world. Singing, which may interact in a variety of ways with the spoken word and with symbolic action, can encourage responsive engagement with issues of peace and social justice.

The flexibility offered by the Church of England's *Common Worship*, and indeed by liturgical renewal in other traditions, enables music to be used in a variety of ways: hymns, songs, psalms, canticles, acclamations, gathering chants, for example. There is scope for creative ways of incorporating music into times of confession, intercessory prayer and statements of faith, and we hope that people using this book will take the opportunity to explore the imaginative liturgical use of some of the shorter musical items we have included. In all-age worship or contexts where English is not the first language for all the congregation, short songs or longer pieces with a refrain can play a valuable role. In some kinds of service, it is appropriate for the congregation to move to different parts of the building, or indeed to be outside at some point (on Palm Sunday, for example) — some of the music provided here will be useful in these situations.

Assisted by having the Church of England's National Worship Development Officer as part of our team, we have considered the full range of liturgical material published as part of the *Common Worship* project, aiming to provide a resource to help those who plan and lead a variety of services. The hymns include several which paraphrase passages of Scripture, from the Psalms and elsewhere, and we have identified those given a particular title (as canticles) in publications such as *Common Worship: Daily Prayer* and *Times and Seasons*. These help to promote biblical literacy and understanding, and the use of metrical paraphrases is worthy of consideration alongside various ways of chanting scriptural texts.

While the needs of Anglican congregations have been a primary focus, we trust that *Sing Praise* will be a valuable resource for other churches too. Contact with songs from the world church, with the work of a new generation of Roman Catholic composers, with music — often folk-song based — from the ecumenical Iona Community (linked with the Church of Scotland) or with the sung prayer of the Taizé Community (founded by a Protestant pastor but now including brothers from many churches and traditions) has been a source of delight and refreshment to many in recent decades. The cross-fertilization of musical traditions has been remarkable in many ways. The contents of this book reflect ecumenical breadth as well as the diversity within what the present Archbishop of Canterbury has called today's 'mixed economy church'.

We felt it important that the book should be structured thematically, for the most part following the broad outline of its immediate predecessor, *Common Praise* (Canterbury Press, 2000). However, since *Sing Praise* is designed as a supplement rather than a comprehensive hymn book in its own right, we have not felt bound to include every category represented there. For example, while there are general hymns celebrating the saints of God, there is nothing related to specific saints' days. Among the supplementary material at the back of the *Full Music* edition we have included both a biblical and a thematic index — neither can be fully comprehensive. It may therefore be helpful, for example, not only to look up the relevant passage in the biblical index but also to refer to 'healing' in the thematic index when choosing music for a service at which the Gospel reading recounts one of Christ's healing miracles.

The ordering of part of the book reflects the underlying shape of many acts of worship, with music for the gathering followed by material relating to penitence, the liturgy of the word, prayer, Holy Communion, and the sending out or dismissal. We have tried to use cross-referencing to give further pointers to how some items might be used — for example, by referring to Gospel acclamations with seasonal verses.

We have kept the interests of choirs in mind, although constraints of space and layout have prevented us from including as many choral arrangements as we might have wished. Many churches have a less traditional musical ensemble instead of or in addition to a choir, and there is music here for them too, as well as for congregations with very limited musical resources — the unaccompanied singing of a short musical unit, perhaps led by a solo voice with others responding, can enrich worship in many different contexts and requires only confidence and imagination. A training scheme for cantors forms part of the RSCM's Church Music Skills programme, and repertoire which can be enhanced by the use of one or more cantors is well represented in *Sing Praise*.

We aimed on the whole for a comfortable pitch for congregational singing, rather than giving the needs of choirs the highest priority. In this we have followed the example of Ralph Vaughan Williams when he chose and edited the music for *The English Hymnal* (1906). We have not entirely avoided keys with a large number of sharps or flats, although these present certain challenges to organists and pianists. In some cases changing the key would have significantly altered what we felt was the appropriate 'colour' of a tune, but we have tried not to ignore the needs of accompanists. Sometimes guitar chords are provided in a more comfortable key, with a 'Capo' indication. In general, guitar and keyboard accompaniments are compatible, even where the chord symbols do not represent every harmonic change in the keyboard part.

Although this collection was originally conceived to complement *Common Praise*, a small proportion of the hymns and songs which we have included are also in the earlier book (sometimes, in the case of hymn texts, with different tunes). These were felt to be items which churches using other mainstream hymn books might well wish to have available in a supplement. It is our hope that *Sing Praise* will find a home in many different contexts, in schools as well as in churches, and that it may help to provide a richer diversity of subject matter and musical styles in those places where predominantly new songs are sung, as well as in more traditional settings. Among the hymns will be found a small number which could not, by any stretch of the imagination, be called 'new', and which are included either because they serve particular needs, or because they are well known only in certain church traditions and, though popular, are not always to be found in mainstream hymn books.

Given the extraordinary diversity of God's creation, we should be cautious about musical homogeneity in worship, of whatever style: might we not rather explore how the use of greater musical diversity could help us to acknowledge the varying ages, ethnicity and musical tastes of our congregations (and visitors) as well as to enrich our experience of the liturgical year? As the musical needs of the Church change from time to time, there is a responsibility in each generation to sift the new material which emerges; some will be discarded, but some may be added to the rich tradition which we pass on to those who follow us. Michael Hawn, writing in a recent issue of the RSCM's magazine, *Church Music Quarterly*, pointed out that if we concentrate only on what we know and love, we leave little space for 'the prophetic word'. Musicians and other leaders of worship, both lay and ordained, are encouraged to explore the contents of this book and to reflect on 'refreshing worship' in their own context, praying for wisdom and discernment.

ANNE HARRISON (Chair), JOHN BARNARD, MICHAEL HAMPEL, PETER MOGER, PETER NARDONE, TIM RUFFER, CHRISTINE SMITH

Cross references

Short lists of hymns and songs also suitable for many of the sections of the book are to be found in the *Full Music* and *Words* editions, and references to alternative tunes for hymns are found in the *Full Music* edition.

Copyright

We are aware that some will want to reproduce material published here, either by printing in congregational service sheets or by projecting on to a screen during worship, and to assist in this process a downloadable electronic words edition is being produced. Much of the music in the book and most of the words are covered by the provisions of one of the two copyright licensing schemes set up to help churches comply with the law: details of the Calamus licence, run by Decani Music, and of Christian Copyright Licensing International can be found by following links on the website associated with this publication (www.singpraise.info). We hope to provide information there on which items are currently covered by which licence.

Publisher's note

The Publishers thank the owners or controllers of copyright for permission to use the hymns and tunes throughout this collection. Where a copyright text has been altered with permission this is denoted with an asterisk before a name, or by the abbreviation *'alt.'* where the author deemed an asterisk unsatisfactory. Acknowledgements are given on-page with the material.

Every effort has been made to trace copyright owners or controllers, to seek permission to use text and music, and to make alterations as necessary. The Publishers apologise to those who have not been traced at the time of going to press, and whose rights have inadvertently not been acknowledged. Any omissions or inaccuracies of permissions or copyright details will be corrected in future printings.

For permission to reproduce copyright hymns and music from this collection, whether in permanent or temporary form, by whatever means, application must be made to the respective owners or controllers at the contact addresses shown on-page.

HYMNS and SONGS

MORNING

BOLNHURST   LM

1   Lord, as I wake I turn to you,
       yourself the first thought of my day:
   my King, my God, whose help is sure,
       yourself the help for which I pray.

2   There is no blessing, Lord, from you
       for those who make their will their way,
   no praise for those who will not praise,
       no peace for those who will not pray.

3   Your loving gifts of grace to me,
       those favours I could never earn,
   call for my thanks in praise and prayer,
       call me to love you in return.

4   Lord, make my life a life of love,
       keep me from sin in all I do;
   Lord, make your law my only law,
       your will my will, for love of you.

BRIAN FOLEY (1919–2000)
based on Psalm 5

Music: PAUL EDWARDS (b. 1955)

1   Words: © 1971, Faber Music Ltd, 3 Queen Square, London. WC1N 3AU
Reprinted from *New Catholic Hymnal* by permission of the publishers.
1   Music: © Paul Edwards / Jubilate Hymns. Administered by The Jubilate Group, 4 Thorne Park Road, Torquay TQ2 6RX
\<copyrightmanager@jubilate.co.uk>   Used by permission.

SLITHERS OF GOLD   11 10 11 10

1 To - day I a - wake____ and God is be - fore____ me. At

night, as I dreamt,____ he sum-moned the day;_____ for

God ne - ver sleeps,____ but pat-terns the morn - - - ing with

sli - thers of gold____ or glo - ry in grey._____

1   Today I awake and God is before me.
         At night, as I dreamt, he summoned the day;
       for God never sleeps, but patterns the morning
         with slithers of gold or glory in grey.

2   Today I arise and Christ is beside me.
         He walked through the dark to scatter new light.
       Yes, Christ is alive, and beckons his people
         to hope and to heal, resist and invite.

3   Today I affirm the Spirit within me
         at worship and work, in struggle and rest.
       The Spirit inspires all life which is changing
         from fearing to faith, from broken to blessed.

4   Today I enjoy the Trinity round me,
         above and beneath, before and behind;
       the Maker, the Son, the Spirit together —
         they called me to life and call me their friend.

JOHN L. BELL *(b.* 1949)
and GRAHAM MAULE *(b.* 1958)

Music: JOHN L. BELL *(b.* 1949)

2   Words: From *Love From Below,* 1989. © 1989, Wild Goose Resource Group,
The Iona Community, 4th Floor, Savoy Centre, 140 Sauchiehall Street, Glasgow G2 3DH
2   Music: From *Love From Below,* 1989. © 1989, Wild Goose Resource Group,
The Iona Community, 4th Floor, Savoy Centre, 140 Sauchiehall Street, Glasgow G2 3DH

EVENING

JACOB

LM

1   Eternal light, shine in my heart;
      eternal hope, lift up my eyes:
     eternal power, be my support;
      eternal wisdom, make me wise.

2   Eternal life, raise me from death;
      eternal brightness, make me see:
     eternal Spirit, give me breath;
      eternal Saviour, come to me:

3   Until by your most costly grace,
      invited by your holy word,
     at last I come before your face
      to know you, my eternal God.

CHRISTOPHER IDLE (*b.* 1938)
based on a prayer of Alcuin of York (*c.* 735–804)

Music: JANE MARSHALL (*b.* 1924)

QUEM PASTORES 888 7

1   Light of gladness, Lord of glory,
        Jesus Christ our king most holy,
        shine among us in your mercy:
           earth and heaven join their hymn.

2   Let us sing at sun's descending
        as we see the lights of evening,
        Father, Son, and Spirit praising
           with the holy seraphim.

3   Son of God, through all the ages
        worthy of our holiest praises,
        yours the life that never ceases,
           light which never shall grow dim.

CHRISTOPHER IDLE (*b.* 1938)
based on *Phos hilaron* (Eastern vesper hymn)

Music: German 15th-century melody
    adapted by RALPH VAUGHAN WILLIAMS (1872–1958)

BLACKHEATH   LM

1   Now as the evening shadows fall,
      God our Creator, hear our call:
     help us to trust your constant grace,
      though darkness seems to hide your face.

2   Help us to find, in sleep's release,
      bodily rest and inner peace;
     so may the darkness of the night
      refresh our eyes for morning light.

3   Father almighty, holy Son,
      Spirit eternal, Three in One,
     grant us the faith that sets us free
      to praise you for eternity.

MICHAEL FORSTER (*b.* 1946)
based on *Te lucis ante terminum*
(Latin, before 11th century)

Music: ANTHONY MILNER (1925–2002)

5   Words: © 1999, Kevin Mayhew Ltd, Buxhall, Stowmarket, Suffolk IP14 3BW   Used by permission.

5   Music: © McCrimmon Publishing Company Limited, 10-12 High Street, Great Wakering, Essex SS3 0EQ.
Used by permission.

GONFALON ROYAL   LM

A - - - men.

1   We praise you, Father, for your gift
         of dusk and nightfall over earth,
     foreshadowing the mystery
         of death that leads to endless day.

2   Within your hands we rest secure;
         in quiet sleep our strength renew;
     yet give your people hearts that wake
         in love to you, unsleeping Lord.

3   Your glory may we ever seek
         in rest, as in activity,
     until its fullness is revealed,
         O source of life, O Trinity. Amen.

St Mary's Abbey, West Malling

Music: PERCY CARTER BUCK (1871–1947)

ADVENT

ANGEL VOICES   85 85 87

For lighting candles on an Advent wreath

Advent 1

1   Advent candles tell their story
      as we watch and pray;
   longing for the Day of Glory,
      'Come, Lord, soon,' we say.
   Pain and sorrow, tears and sadness
      changed for gladness on that Day.

Advent 2

2   Prophet voices loudly crying,
      making pathways clear;
   glimpsing glory, self-denying,
      calling all to hear.
   Through their message — challenged, shaken —
      hearts awaken: God is near!

Music: EDWIN GEORGE MONK (1819–1900)

Advent 3

3 John the Baptist, by his preaching
   and by water poured,
brought to those who heard his teaching
   news of hope restored:
'Keep your vision strong and steady,
   and be ready for the Lord.'

Advent 4

4 Mary's gift beyond all telling
   we recall today:
Son of God within her dwelling,
   born to show the way.
Who could guess the final story?
   — cross and glory; Easter Day!

Christmas Day

5 Advent candles tell their story
   on this Christmas Day.
Those who waited for God's glory:
   they prepared the way.
Christ is with us: loving, giving,
   in us living, here today!

MARK EAREY (b. 1965)

MARCHING THROUGH GEORGIA   13 13 13 8 and refrain

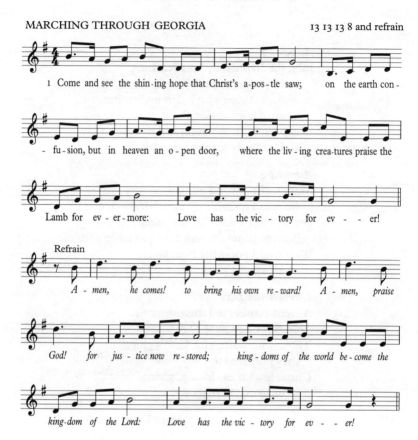

1 Come and see the shin-ing hope that Christ's a-pos-tle saw; on the earth con-
fu-sion, but in heaven an o-pen door, where the liv-ing crea-tures praise the
Lamb for ev-er-more: Love has the vic-tory for ev - - er!

Refrain

A - men, he comes! to bring his own re-ward! A - men, praise
God! for jus-tice now re-stored; king-doms of the world be-come the
king-dom of the Lord: Love has the vic-tory for ev - - er!

Music: HENRY CLAY WORK (1832–1884)
arranged by DAVID WILSON (b. 1940)

1   Come and see the shining hope that Christ's apostle saw;
on the earth confusion, but in heaven an open door,
where the living creatures praise the Lamb for evermore:
    Love has the victory for ever!

    Amen, he comes! to bring his own reward!
    Amen, praise God! for justice now restored;
    kingdoms of the world become the kingdom of the Lord:
      Love has the victory for ever!

2   All the gifts you send us, Lord, are faithful, good, and true;
holiness and righteousness are shown in all you do:
who can see your greatest Gift and fail to worship you?
    Love has the victory for ever!

3   Power and salvation all belong to God on high!
So the mighty multitudes of heaven make their cry,
singing Alleluia! where the echoes never die:
    Love has the victory for ever!

CHRISTOPHER IDLE (*b.* 1938)
based on Revelation 4, 5, 15

INVOCATIONS

10 9 6 6 10

1 Come, light of the world, light up our lives, Lord; come, light of the world, light up our hearts. Dis-pel all our dark-ness, re-move all our blind-ness; come, light of the world, be light for our eyes.

Music: PAUL INWOOD (*b.* 1947)

1   Come, light of the world, light up our lives, Lord;
    come, light of the world, light up our hearts.
      Dispel all our darkness,
      remove all our blindness;
    come, light of the world, be light for our eyes.

2   Come, strength of our days, strengthen our lives, Lord;
    come, strength of our days, strengthen our hearts.
      Come, fill us with courage
      to follow you always;
    come, strength of our days, be strength for our minds.

3   Come, joy for the world, fill us with gladness;
    come, joy for the world, gladden our hearts.
      Come, bring us together
      with singing and laughter;
    come, joy for the world, bring warmth to our lives.

4   Come, hope of the world, comfort your people;
    come, hope of the world, comfort our hearts.
      Come, heal all our sorrow
      with love and compassion;
    come, hope of the world, bring peace to us all.

5   Come, Spirit of God, be with us now, Lord;
    come, Spirit of God, fill us with truth.
      Enlighten our lives, Lord,
      with radiance and power;
    come, Spirit of God, inspire all we do.

PAUL INWOOD (b. 1947)

9 Words and Music: © 1990 Paul Inwood, admin. World Library Publications. Permission applied for.

O-SO-SO   65 56

Gently

1   Come now, O Prince of Peace,
   make us one body,
    come, O Lord Jesus,
  reconcile your people.

2   Come now, O God of love,
   make us one body,
    come, O Lord Jesus,
  reconcile your people.

3   Come now and set us free,
   O God, our Saviour,
    come, O Lord Jesus,
  reconcile all nations.

4   Come, Hope of unity,
   make us one body,
    come, O Lord Jesus,
  reconcile all nations.

GEONYONG LEE
revised by MARION POPE

Music: GEONYONG LEE

CRUCIFER   10 10 and refrain

Fling wide the gates, unbar the ancient doors;
salute your king in his triumphant cause!

1   Now all the world belongs to Christ our Lord:
     let all creation greet the living Word!

2   Who has the right to worship him today?
     All those who gladly serve him and obey.

3   He comes to save all those who trust his name,
     and will declare them free from guilt and shame.

4   Who is the victor glorious from the fight?
     He is our king , our life, our Lord, our right!

MICHAEL PERRY (1942–1996)
based on Psalm 24 *(A Song of the King's Glory)*

Music: SYDNEY HUGO NICHOLSON (1875–1947)

1 In-to the dark-ness of this world,—
2 In-to the long-ing of our souls,—
3 O Ho-ly Child,— Em-ma-nu-el,—

in-to the sha-dows of the night, in-to this love-less
in-to these hea-vy hearts of stone, shine on us now— your
Hope of the a-ges, God with us, vi-sit a-gain— this

place you came,— light-ened our bur-den, eased our pain,— and
pier-cing light,— or-der our lives— and souls a-right,— by
bro-ken place,— till all the earth— de-clare your praise— and

made these hearts your home.— In-to the dark-ness
grace and love un-known,— un-til in you— our
your great mer-cies own.— Now let your love— be

Refrain

once a-gain,— O come, Lord Je-sus, come.— (1,2) *Come with your love—*
hearts u-nite,— O come, Lord Je-sus, come.— (3) *Come in your glo-*
born in us— O come, Lord Je-sus, come.—

— to make— us whole,— come with your light— to lead— us on,—
— -ry, take— your place,— Je-sus the Name— a-bove— all names,

— driv-ing the dark--ness far from our souls:— O
— we long to see— you face— to face:— O

v. 3

come, Lord Je-sus, come.—
come, Lord Je-sus, come.—

MAGGI DAWN (b.1959)

Music: MAGGI DAWN (b.1959)

CHRIST BE OUR LIGHT

Unison

1 Long-ing for light,— we wait in dark-ness. Long-ing for
truth,— we turn to you. Make us your own,—
your ho-ly peo-ple, light for the world to see.—

Refrain

Christ, be our light! Shine in our hearts.
Shine through the dark - - ness. Christ, be our light!

Fine

Shine in your Church gath-ered to - day.—

For a descant to the refrain see 73.

2 Longing for peace, our world is troubled.
Longing for hope, many despair.
Your word alone has power to save us.
Make us your living voice.

3 Longing for food, many are hungry.
Longing for water, many still thirst.
Make us your bread, broken for others,
shared until all are fed.

4 Longing for shelter, many are homeless.
Longing for warmth, many are cold.
Make us your building, sheltering others,
walls made of living stone.

5 Many the gifts, many the people,
many the hearts that yearn to belong.
Let us be servants to one another,
making your kingdom come.

BERNADETTE FARRELL (b. 1957)

Music: BERNADETTE FARRELL (b. 1957)

ST THOMAS   SM

VENICE   SM

1   O Child of promise, come!
       O come, Emmanuel!
   Come, Prince of Peace, to David's throne;
     come, God, with us to dwell.

2   The Lord's true Servant, come,
     in whom is his delight,
   on whom his Holy Spirit rests,
     the Gentiles' promised light.

3   O come, Anointed One,
     to show blind eyes your face!
   Good tidings to the poor announce;
     proclaim God's year of grace!

4   O come, Messiah King,
     to reign in endless light,
   when heavenly peace at last goes forth
     from Sion's holy height.

JAMES QUINN, SJ   (1919–2010)

Music: 1: From Aaron Williams: *New Universal Psalmodist,* 1770
Music: 2: WILLIAM AMPS (1824–1910)

BESANÇON CAROL · 87 98 87

Unison

1   People, look east to see at last
      hopes fulfilled from ages past:
    now in the promise of the morning,
      see, a brighter day is dawning,
    rich with the visions long foretold,
      prophets' dreams from days of old.

2   God reaffirms the gracious call:
      words of welcome meant for all;
    comfort enough for all our sorrows;
      justice shaping new tomorrows.
    Mercy bears fruit in lives restored,
      freed to praise and serve the Lord.

3   Now, with the coming of the light,
      darkest fears are put to flight;
    see how the clouds of gloom are clearing,
      blown aside by hope's appearing.
    Jesus, the Light of all our days,
      comes and sets our hearts ablaze.

4   Born of our race, a child so small —
      hail the promised Lord of all!
    Nailed to a cross for our salvation,
      he shall rule God's new creation.
    Lift up your eyes, and look again:
      see, he comes in power to reign!

MARTIN LECKEBUSCH (*b.* 1962)

Music: French traditional carol
  harmonised by MARTIN SHAW (1875–1958)

POWERSTOCK   11 11 6 6

1   Sing we of the Kingdom, giving thanks to God,
    sing we of the advent of the Son of God.
      Enable me, truly,
       to live my life for God.

2   Sing we of the Baptist, giving thanks to God,
    sing we of his mission and his life for God.
      Enable me, truly,
       to live my life for God.

3   Sing we now of Mary, giving thanks to God,
    sing we of her lowliness and love for God.
      Enable me, truly,
       to live my life for God.

4   Sing we now of Jesus, giving thanks to God,
    sing we of his life and of the love bestowed,
      enabling me, truly,
       to live my life for God.

PETER NARDONE   *(b. 1965)*

Music: PETER NARDONE *(b. 1965)*

17

ST JOHN DAMASCENE   76 76 D

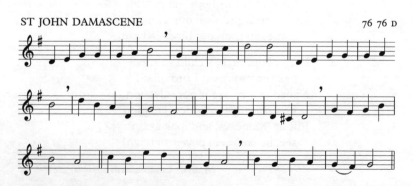

Music: ARTHUR HENRY BROWN *(1830–1926)*

1   When the King shall come again
      all his power revealing,
   splendour shall announce his reign,
      life and joy and healing:
   earth no longer in decay,
      hope no more frustrated;
   this is God's redemption-day
      longingly awaited.

2   In the desert trees take root
      fresh from his creation;
   plants and flowers and sweetest fruit
      join the celebration:
   rivers spring up from the earth,
      barren lands adorning;
   valleys, this is your new birth,
      mountains, greet the morning!

3   Strengthen feeble hands and knees,
      fainting hearts, be cheerful!
   God who comes for such as these
      seeks and saves the fearful:
   deaf ears hear the silent tongues
      sing away their weeping;
   blind eyes see the lifeless ones
      walking, running, leaping.

4   There God's highway shall be seen
      where no roaring lion,
   nothing evil or unclean
      walks the road to Zion:
   ransomed people homeward bound,
      all your praises voicing,
   see your Lord with glory crowned,
      share in his rejoicing!

CHRISTOPHER IDLE (b. 1938)
based on Isaiah 35

Cantor (or group)

1 Pre - pare the way for the Lord. Make a straight path for God.

2 Re-joice in the Lord al - ways: God is at hand.

3 The glo-ry of the

Ostinato

Wait for the Lord, whose day is near.

(Continues on opposite page.)

vv. 4 - 7

4 I

6 Seek

Ostinato

Wait for the Lord, whose day is near.

*Some or all of the optional verses, for one or more cantors, may be added once the
ostinato has been sung at least twice.*

Music: JACQUES BERTHIER (1923–1994)

ADVENT

Pre-pare the way for the Lord.

Joy and glad-ness for all who seek the Lord.

Lord shall be re-vealed. All the earth will see the Lord.

Wait for the Lord: keep watch, take heart!

wait-ed for the Lord. God heard my cry.

5 Our eyes are fixed on the Lord our God.

first the king-dom of God. Seek and you shall find.

7 O Lord, show us your way. Guide us in your truth.

Fine

Wait for the Lord: keep watch, take heart!

Taizé Community

Psalm 27.14, Isaiah 40.3, Philippians 4.4-5, Psalm 70.4, Isaiah 40.5,
Psalm 38.15, Psalm 123.2, Matthew 6.33, 7.7, Psalm 86.11

LITANY OF THE WORD

1 Word of jus - tice, al - le - lu - ia, come to dwell here. Ma - ran - a - tha!

2 Word of mercy, alleluia,
    live among us. Maranatha!

3 Word of power, alleluia,
    live within us. Maranatha!

4 Word of freedom, alleluia,
    save your people. Maranatha!

5 Word of healing, alleluia,
    heal our sorrow. Maranatha!

6 Word of comfort, alleluia,
    bring us hope now. Maranatha!

7 Word of gladness, alleluia,
    fill our hearts now. Maranatha!

8 Word of wisdom, alleluia,
    come, renew us. Maranatha!

9 Word we long for, alleluia,
    Word we thirst for. Maranatha!

10 Key of David, alleluia,
     Son of Mary. Maranatha!

11 Cry of prophets, alleluia,
     hope of ages. Maranatha!

12 Light of nations, alleluia,
     light in darkness. Maranatha!

BERNADETTE FARRELL (b. 1957)

'Maranatha' means 'Our Lord, come.'

Music: BERNADETTE FARRELL (b. 1957)

MARSTON ST LAWRENCE 77 77 3

Descant (v. 4)

4 Lift your hearts and voi - ces high: then shall glo - ry fill the

Unison

sky — Christ shall come and not be long, earth shall

sing the an - gels' song: 'Glo - - - ri - a!'

1 Lift your heart and raise your voice,
     faithful people, come, rejoice:
   grace and power are shown on earth
     in the Saviour's holy birth.
       Gloria!

2 Mortals, hear what angels say;
     shepherds, quickly make your way,
   finding truth in lowly guise,
     wisdom to confound the wise.
       Gloria!

3 Here he lies, the Lord of all;
     nature's king in cattle-stall,
   God of heaven to earth come down —
     cross for throne and thorn for crown.
       Gloria!

4 Lift your hearts and voices high:
     then shall glory fill the sky —
   Christ shall come and not be long,
     earth shall sing the angels' song:
       'Gloria!'

Music: PAUL EDWARDS (b. 1955)   MICHAEL PERRY (1942–1996)

Softly, with awe

1 Like a can-dle flame, flicker-ing small in our dark-ness,

un - -cre - - a -ted light shines through in - fant eyes.

Refrain

Women

Men

God is with us, al - le -

God is with us, al - le - - lu - - ia,

- lu - - ia,   come to save us, al - le - lu - -

come to save us, al - le - - lu - - ia,   al - le - lu - -

vv. 1,2   *v. 3*   D.S.   Last time

ia. _____   *- ia.*   *- ia.*

2   Stars and angels sing,
     yet the earth sleeps in shadows;
     can this tiny spark set a world on fire?

3   Yet his light shall shine
     from our lives, Spirit blazing,
     as we touch the flame of his holy fire.

GRAHAM KENDRICK   (*b.* 1950)

Music: GRAHAM KENDRICK (*b.* 1950)

21   Words and Music: © 1988, Graham Kendrick / Make Way Music Ltd, PO Box 320, Tunbridge Wells, Kent.
TN2 9DE UK. <www.grahamkendrick.co.uk> Used by permission.

SCARLET RIBBONS   87 87 D

1   Who would think that what was needed
        to transform and save the earth
     might not be a plan or army
        proud in purpose, proved in worth?
     Who would think, despite derision,
        that a child should lead the way?
     God surprises earth with heaven,
        coming here on Christmas Day.

2   Shepherds watch and wise men wonder,
        monarchs scorn and angels sing;
     such a place as none would reckon
        hosts a holy, helpless thing;
     stabled beasts and bypassed strangers
        watch a baby laid in hay:
     God surprises earth with heaven,
        coming here on Christmas Day.

3   Centuries of skill and science
        span the past from which we move,
     yet experience questions whether
        with such progress we improve.
     While the human lot we ponder,
        lest our hopes and humour fray,
     God surprises earth with heaven,
        coming here on Christmas Day.

JOHN L. BELL (b. 1949)
and GRAHAM MAULE (b. 1958)

Music: EVELYN DANZIG (1901–1996)
arranged by JOHN L. BELL (b. 1949)

22   Words: From *Heaven Shall Not Wait*, 1987. © 1987, Wild Goose Resource Group,
The Iona Community, 4th Floor, Savoy Centre, 140 Sauchiehall Street, Glasgow G2 3DH

22   Music: © 1949 (Renewed) EMI Mills Music Inc. All rights controlled by EMI Mills Music Inc. (Publishing)
and Alfred Music Publishing Co. Inc. (Print). All rights reserved. Used by permission.

Music: 1: DONALD DAVISON (*b.* 1937)

Music: 2: English traditional melody

Adapted by RALPH VAUGHAN WILLIAMS (1872–1958)

The Massacre of the Innocents

1   In the night, the sound of crying —
      whimpers from a babe so small:
    angels hail the new-born infant
      in that dingy cattle-stall.

2   In the night, the sound of crying —
      Mary journeys on with tears,
    further from the home she treasures,
      onward to uncertain years.

3   In the night, the sound of crying —
      fury nothing can assuage!
    Schemes of pointless, brutal murder
      spring from Herod's jealous rage.

4   In the night, the sound of crying —
      agonies beyond belief!
    Soldiers searching, children slaughtered —
      parents overwhelmed with grief.

5   In the night, the sound of crying —
      cries of faith, though hope looks vain;
    cries of joy, for Christ has conquered,
      and, with justice, comes to reign.

MARTIN LECKEBUSCH   (b. 1962)

CHRISTINGLE

THE HOLLY AND THE IVY   76 87 and refrain

Unison

Refrain, Harmony

1   It's rounded like an orange,
    this earth on which we stand;
    and we praise the God who holds it
    in the hollow of his hand.
    So, Father, we would thank you
    for all that you have done,
    and for all that you have given us
    through the coming of your Son.

2   A candle, burning brightly,
    can cheer the darkest night,
    and these candles tell how Jesus
    came to bring a dark world light.

3   The ribbon round the orange
    reminds us of the cost;
    how the Shepherd, strong and gentle,
    gave his life to save the lost.

4   Four seasons with their harvest
    supply the food we need,
    and the Spirit gives a harvest
    that can make us rich indeed.

5   We come with our Christingles
    to tell of Jesus' birth,
    and we praise the God who blessed us
    by his coming to this earth.

Music: Old English carol   BASIL BRIDGE *(b.1927)*
    harmonised by Compilers of *Church Hymnary,* 4th edition, 2005

EPIPHANY

CHURCH TRIUMPHANT   LM

1   Arise, shine out, your light has come,
      unfolding City of our dreams.
    On distant hills a glory gleams:
      the new creation has begun.

2   Above earth's valleys, thick with night,
      high on your walls the dawn appears,
    and history shall dry its tears,
      as nations stream towards your light.

3   From walls surpassing time and space,
      unnumbered gates, like open hands,
    shall gather gifts from all the lands,
      and welcome all the human race.

4   The sounds of violence shall cease
      as dwellings of salvation rise
    to sparkle in eternal skies
      from avenues of praise and peace.

5   The dancing air shall glow with light
      and sun and moon give up their place
    when Love shines out of every face:
      our Good, our Glory, our Delight.

BRIAN WREN *(b.1936)*
based on Isaiah 60 *(A Song of the New Jerusalem)*

Music: JAMES WILLIAM ELLIOTT (1833–1915)

GODMANCHESTER

10 10 10 10

1   Christ is our light! the bright and morning star
covering with radiance all from near and far.
    Christ be our light, shine on, shine on we pray
into our hearts, into our world today.

2   Christ is our love! baptized that we may know
the love of God among us, swooping low.
    Christ be our love, bring us to turn our face
and see you in the light of heaven's embrace.

3   Christ is our joy! transforming wedding guest!
Through water turned to wine the feast was blessed.
    Christ be our joy; your glory let us see,
as your disciples did in Galilee.

Music: PETER MOGER (*b.* 1964)

LEITH FISHER (1941–2009)

27

UPTON CHEYNEY

74 74 D

Music: JOHN BARNARD (*b.* 1948)

1   In our darkness light has shone,
        Alleluia,
    still today the light shines on,
        Alleluia;
    Word made flesh in human birth,
        Alleluia,
    Light and Life of all the earth,
        Alleluia!

2   Christ the Son incarnate see,
        Alleluia,
    by whom all things came to be,
        Alleluia;
    through the world his splendours shine,
        Alleluia,
    full of grace and truth divine,
        Alleluia!

3   All who now in him believe,
        Alleluia,
    everlasting life receive,
        Alleluia;
    born of God and in his care,
        Alleluia,
    we his name and nature share,
        Alleluia!

4   Christ a child on earth appears,
        Alleluia,
    crown of all creation's years,
        Alleluia;
    God's eternal Word has come,
        Alleluia,
    he shall lead his people home,
        Alleluia!

TIMOTHY DUDLEY-SMITH (b. 1926)
based on John 1.1-14

UNSER HERRSCHER (NEANDER)   87 87 87

1   Jesus, come! for we invite you,
          Guest and Master, Friend and Lord;
      now, as once at Cana's wedding,
          speak, and let us hear your word:
      lead us through our need or doubting,
          hope be born and joy restored.

2   Jesus, come! transform our pleasures,
          guide us into paths unknown;
      bring your gifts, command your servants,
          let us trust in you alone:
      though your hand may work in secret,
          all shall see what you have done.

3   Jesus, come in new creation,
          heaven brought near in power divine;
      give your unexpected glory
          changing water into wine:
      rouse the faith of your disciples —
          come, our first and greatest Sign!

4   Jesus, come! surprise our dullness,
          make us willing to receive
      more than we can yet imagine,
          all the best you have to give:
      let us find your hidden riches,
          taste your love, believe, and live!

CHRISTOPHER IDLE (b. 1938)
based on John 2.1-4

Music: Melody set to *Unser Herrscher* in *Alpha und Omega*
JOACHIM NEANDER (1650–1680)

BREMEN (NEUMARK)   98 98 88

1   Wise men, they came to look for wisdom,
    finding one wiser than they knew;
  rich men, they met with one yet richer —
    King of the kings, they knelt to you:
    Jesus, our wisdom from above,
    wealth and redemption, life and love.

2   Pilgrims they were, from unknown countries,
    searching for one who knows the world;
  lost are their names, and strange their journeys,
    famed is their zeal to find the child:
    Jesus, in you the lost are claimed,
    strangers are found, and known, and named.

3   Magi, they stooped to see your splendour,
    led by a star to light supreme;
  promised Messiah, Lord eternal,
    glory and peace are in your name.
    Joy of each day, our song by night,
    shine on our path your holy light.

4   Guests of their God, they opened treasures,
    incense and gold and solemn myrrh,
  welcoming one too young to question
    how came these gifts, and what they were.
    Gift beyond price of gold or gem,
    make among us your Bethlehem.

CHRISTOPHER IDLE (b. 1938)

Music: Melody by GEORG NEUMARK (1621–1681)
    in *Fortgepflantzter Musikalisch-Poetischer Lustwald*, 1657
    arranged by ERIK ROUTLEY (1917–1982)

THE BAPTISM of CHRIST

SOLOTHURN

LM

1 The sinless one to Jordan came
   to share our fallen nature's blame;
   God's righteousness he thus fulfilled
   and chose the path his Father willed.

2 Uprising from the waters there,
   the voice from heaven did witness bear
   that he, the Son of God, had come
   to lead his scattered people home.

3 Above him see the heavenly Dove,
   the sign of God the Father's love,
   now by the Holy Spirit shed
   upon the Son's anointed head.

4 How blessed that mission then begun
   to heal and save a race undone;
   straight to the wilderness he goes
   to wrestle with his people's foes.

5 Dear Lord, let those baptized from sin
   go forth with you, a world to win;
   and send the Holy Spirit's power
   to shield them in temptation's hour.

6 On you shall all your people feed
   and know you are the Bread indeed,
   who gives eternal life to those
   that with you died, and with you rose.

GEORGE B. TIMMS (1910–1997)

Music: Swiss traditional melody in Reichart's *Frohe Lieder für deutsche Männer*, 1781, *arranged by* Compilers of *Common Praise*, 2000

HERONGATE   LM

1   When Jesus comes to be baptized,
         he leaves the hidden years behind,
     the years of safety and of peace,
         to bear the sins of humankind.

2   The Spirit of the Lord comes down,
         anoints the Christ to suffering,
     to preach the word, to free the bound,
         and to the mourner comfort bring.

3   He will not quench the dying flame,
         and what is bruised he will not break,
     but heal the wound injustice dealt,
         and out of death his triumph make.

4   Our everlasting Father praise
         with Christ, his well-belovèd Son,
     who with the Spirit reigns serene,
         eternal Trinity in One.

                                  Stanbrook Abbey

Music: English traditional melody
     arranged by RALPH VAUGHAN WILLIAMS (1872–1958)

THE PRESENTATION of CHRIST
in the TEMPLE

VASEY

886 D

1 Light of the world, true light di-vine,— in glo-ry break and splen-dour shine— up-on our na-ture's— night! The dark-ness dies be-fore the morn— and God him-self a child is born,— the long-a-wait-ed— Light.

2 Life of the world, a life laid down, who chose the cross be-fore the crown and— op-ened heav-en's— door: he broke the chains of death and hell,— our Sa-viour Christ, Em-ma-nu-el,— who lives for ev-er-more.

3 Lord of all worlds, a man-ger bed— was room e-nough to lay your head— when, from your throne a-bove, you came to set a lost world right,— im-mor-tal Life, un-fad-ing Light, and all-pre-vail-ing—

vv. 1,2

v. 3

Love.

Im-mor-tal Life, un-fad-ing Light,— and all-pre-vail-ing— Love.

TIMOTHY DUDLEY-SMITH (b. 1926)

Music: ANNE HARRISON (b. 1954)

WEST ASHTON   10 10 10 10

1   New light has dawned, the Son of God is here,
        a holy light no earthly light outshines;
    the light has dawned, the light that casts out fear,
        the light that evil dreads and love defines.

2   The light of glory shines to angels' song,
        the shepherds run to where a baby lies;
    a servant of the Lord, who waited long,
        acclaims the light to lighten Gentile eyes.

3   And priestly men sit listening to a boy,
        they see the dawning light within his face.
    Such words they hear those Christ-child lips employ!
        Amazing words of wisdom, truth and grace.

4   O Christ, the light who came to us on earth,
        shine through the shadow cast by human sin;
    renew the faith you gave at our new birth,
        destroy the dark, and let your light come in.

PAUL WIGMORE (b. 1925)

Music: JOHN BARNARD (b. 1948)

LENT

ASTON ROWANT

II 10 II 10 D

Music: JOHN BARNARD (*b.* 1948)

1 Above the voices of the world around me,
my hopes and dreams, my cares and loves and fears,
the long-awaited call of Christ has found me,
the voice of Jesus echoes in my ears:
 'I gave my life to break the cords that bind you,
 I rose from death to set your spirit free;
 turn from your sins and put the past behind you,
 take up your cross and come and follow me.'

2 What can I offer him who calls me to him?
Only the wastes of sin and self and shame;
a mind confused, a heart that never knew him,
a tongue unskilled at naming Jesus' name.
 Yet at your call, and hungry for your blessing,
 drawn by that cross which moves a heart of stone,
 now Lord I come, my tale of sin confessing,
 and in repentance turn to you alone.

3 Lord, I believe; help now my unbelieving;
I come in faith because your promise stands.
Your word of pardon and of peace receiving,
all that I am I place within your hands.
 Let me become what you shall choose to make me,
 freed from the guilt and burden of my sins.
 Jesus is mine, who never shall forsake me,
 and in his love my new-born life begins.

TIMOTHY DUDLEY-SMITH (b. 1926)

PORTHOLME   LM

BOW BRICKHILL   LM

Music: 1: PETER MOGER (*b.* 1964)
Music: 2: SYDNEY HUGO NICHOLSON (1875–1947)

1   Forgive us when our deeds ignore
      your righteous rule of all the earth,
   when our decisions harm the poor,
      denying their eternal worth.

2   Forgive us when we turn aside
      from what is honest, true and fair,
   when dreams of pleasure, wealth and pride
      supplant your clear commands to care.

3   Forgive us, Lord, our endless greed
      for what was never truly ours,
   when, driven more by want than need,
      we harness this world's brutal powers.

4   Forgive us that we change the rules
      by which the game of life is played,
   and never learn to wield the tools
      which could see joy and hope remade.

5   Forgive us, God! Our lives betray
      our shallow, vague response to grace;
   so help us walk your holy way,
      to make your world a better place.

MARTIN LECKEBUSCH (b. 1962)

The refrain (with this or the alternative text) may be sung as an ostinato, with verses sung by a cantor or group.

Music: TERESA BROWN (b. 1953)

LENT

From ashes to ashes, from dust to dust,
from life through death to eternal life.
Now is the time to turn from sin,
be faithful once more to your God.

[Alternative refrain:
The God of compassion and love awaits
with tenderness to forgive you now.
Come back to him with all your heart:
receive his mercy and love.]

Cantor(s) or all:

1 God the Father created you,
    he loves you, he calls to you now.
   So patiently he waits for you
    to turn back to him once again.

2 Stay awake and be ready,
    for you know not the day nor the hour.
   Remember the words of Jesus Christ:
    'Repent and believe the good news.'

3 Holy Spirit of God,
    renew in us your power and love.
   Come guide our hearts and minds today,
    that we may repent and believe.

TERESA BROWN (*b.* 1953)

BANGOR   CM

1   From ashes to the living font
        your Church must journey, Lord,
     baptized in grace, in grace renewed
        by your most holy word.

2   Through fasting, prayer and charity
        your voice speaks deep within,
     returning us to ways of truth
        and turning us from sin.

3   From desert to the mountaintop
        in Christ our way we see,
     so, tempered by temptation's might,
        we might transfigured be.

4   For thirsting hearts let water flow,
        our fainting souls revive;
     and at the well your waters give
        our everlasting life.

5   From ashes to the living font
        your Church must journey still;
     through cross and tomb to Easter joy,
        in Spirit-fire fulfilled.

ALAN J. HOMMERDING (*b.* 1956)

Music: Melody from William Tans'ur's *Harmony of Syon* 1735

BRESLAU   LM

1 From the deep places, hear my cry,
      those hidden depths of guilt within:
   O God of mercy, God Most High,
      keep no account of all my sin.

2 Before your glory none can stand,
      no mortal eye behold your face:
   extend to me your kingly hand,
      the sovereign touch of saving grace.

3 O Lord, in whom all needs are met,
      draw near in love to me, I pray,
   for on your word my hopes are set,
      as watchmen wait for coming day.

4 As watchmen wait till dawn appears,
      so God's redeeming love is shown;
   to shed, unfailing through the years,
      the dew of blessing on his own.

TIMOTHY DUDLEY-SMITH (b. 1926)
based on Psalm 130

Music: German, 15th century, as adapted in *As hymnodus sacer*, Leipzig,
1625, *harmonised by* FELIX MENDELSSOHN-BARTHOLDY (1809–1847)

THE TRUTH FROM ABOVE   LM

Music: English traditional melody
Harmony adapted from *Fantasia on Christmas Carols*
by RALPH VAUGHAN WILLIAMS (1872–1958)

1   Hear me, O Lord, in my distress,
      give ear to my despairing plea!
  In faithfulness, in righteousness,
      O hear my prayer and answer me.

2   I claim no favour as of right;
      you are the God I serve and trust,
  yet judge me not: for in your sight
      no living soul is counted just.

* 3   My fierce oppressor hunts me down:
      I shrink in darkness, like the dead;
  my spirit fails — all hope is gone,
      my heart is overwhelmed with dread.

* 4   Days long since vanished I review,
      I see the wonders of your hands,
  and I stretch out my hands to you,
      for you I thirst like desert sands.

5   Lord, answer me without delay!
      I perish if you hide your face;
  in you I trust: let this new day
      bring word of your unfailing grace.

6   From my pursuers save me still:
      in you my refuge I have found;
  teach me, O God, to do your will,
      and lead my feet on level ground.

7   For your name's sake, Lord, hear my plea:
      your servant's stricken life preserve!
  From all oppression set me free
      to live and love the God I serve.

DAVID G. PRESTON *(b. 1939)*
based on Psalm 143 *(A Song of Entreaty)*

One or more verses may be sung by a solo voice.

SONG 24

10 10 10 10

1　O God, be gracious to me in your love,
　　　and in your mercy pardon my misdeeds;
　　wash me from guilt and cleanse me from my sin,
　　　for well I know the evil I have done.

2　Against you, Lord, you only have I sinned,
　　　and what to you is hateful have I done;
　　I own your righteousness in charging me,
　　　I know you to be just should you condemn.

3　Take hyssop, sprinkle me and make me clean,
　　　wash me and make me whiter than the snow;
　　fill me with gladness and rejoicing, Lord,
　　　and let my broken frame know joy once more.

4　Turn now your face, Lord God, from my misdeeds,
　　　and blot out all the sins that sully me;
　　create a clean and contrite heart in me,
　　　renew my soul in faithfulness and love.

5　Drive me not from your presence, gracious Lord,
　　　nor keep your Holy Spirit far from me;
　　restore my soul with your salvation's joy,
　　　and with a willing spirit strengthen me.

IAN ROBERTSON PITT-WATSON (1923–1995)
based on Psalm 51.1-12 *(A Song of Penitence)*

Music: ORLANDO GIBBONS (1583–1625)

Refrain

Praise to you, O Christ, our Sav-iour, Word of the Fa-ther,
call-ing us to life; Son of God who leads us to free-dom:
To verses | *Last time*
glo-ry to you, Lord Je-sus Christ! Christ!

1 You are the Word who calls us out of dark-ness; you are the Word who
leads us in-to light; you are the Word who brings us through the
D.C.
de - sert: glo - ry to you, Lord Je-sus Christ!

2　　You are the one whom prophets hoped and longed for;
　　　　you are the one who speaks to us today;
　　　you are the one who leads us to our future:
　　　　glory to you, Lord Jesus Christ!

3　　You are the Word who calls us to be servants;
　　　　you are the Word whose only law is love;
　　　you are the Word-made-flesh who lives among us:
　　　　glory to you, Lord Jesus Christ!

4　　You are the Word who binds us and unites us;
　　　　you are the Word who calls us to be one;
　　　you are the Word who teaches us forgiveness:
　　　　glory to you, Lord Jesus Christ!

BERNADETTE FARRELL (*b.* 1957)

Music: BERNADETTE FARRELL (*b.* 1957)

MOTHERING SUNDAY

LOVE DIVINE   87 87

1 God of Eve and God of Mary,
   God of love and mother-earth,
thank you for the ones who with us
   shared their life and gave us birth.

2 As you came to earth in Jesus,
   so you come to us today;
you are present in the caring
   that prepares us for life's way.

3 Thank you that the Church, our Mother,
   gives us bread and fills our cup,
and the comfort of the Spirit
   warms our hearts and lifts us up.

4 Thank you for belonging, shelter,
   bonds of friendship, ties of blood,
and for those who have no children,
   yet are parents under God.

5 God of Eve and God of Mary,
   Christ our brother, human Son,
Spirit, caring like a Mother,
   take our love and make us one!

Music: JOHN STAINER (1840–1901)   FRED KAAN (1929–2009)

43

ELLACOMBE   76 76 D

MOTHERING SUNDAY

1. Our Father God in heaven
   on whom our world depends,
   to you let praise be given
   for families and friends;
   for parents, sisters, brothers,
   a home where love belongs,
   but on this day for mothers
   we bring our thankful songs.

2. What wealth of God's bestowing
   for all the world to share!
   what strength of heart outgoing
   to children everywhere!
   Our deepest joys and sorrows
   a mother's path must trace,
   and earth's unknown tomorrows
   are held in her embrace.

3. How well we know the story
   that tells of Jesus' birth,
   the Lord of heaven's glory
   become a child of earth;
   a helpless infant sleeping,
   yet King of realms above,
   to find in Mary's keeping
   the warmth of human love.

4. Our Father God in heaven,
   to you we lift our prayer,
   that every child be given
   such tenderness and care,
   where life is all for others,
   where love your love displays:
   for God's good gift of mothers
   let earth unite in praise!

TIMOTHY DUDLEY-SMITH (b. 1926)

Music: German melody, 18th century, as adapted in *Gesangbuch*, Mainz, 1833, and harmonised in *Gesangbuch*, St Gallen, 1863

PASSIONTIDE

1 Be-neath the cross of Je - sus I___ find a place to stand, and___ won-der at such mer - cy that___ calls me as I am. For___ hands that should dis--card me hold___ wounds which tell me 'Come.' Be--neath the cross of Je - sus my un-wor-thy soul is

vv. 1,2   *v. 3*

won.   Be - - lives.

2   Beneath the cross of Jesus
        his family is my own —
    once strangers chasing selfish dreams,
        now one through grace alone.
    How could I now dishonour
        the ones that you have loved?
    Beneath the cross of Jesus
        see the children called by God.

3   Beneath the cross of Jesus —
        the path before the crown —
    we follow in his footsteps
        where promised hope is found.
    How great the joy before us
        to be his perfect Bride.
    Beneath the cross of Jesus
        we will gladly live our lives.

KEITH GETTY *(b. 1974)*
and KRISTYN GETTY *(b. 1980)*

Music: KEITH GETTY *(b. 1974)* and KRISTYN GETTY *(b. 1980)*

DIM OND JESU   87 87 D

1   Here is love, vast as the ocean,
        loving kindness as the flood,
     when the Prince of life, our ransom,
        shed for us his precious blood.
     Who his love will not remember?
        Who can cease to sing his praise?
     He can never be forgotten
        throughout heaven's eternal days.

2   On the mount of crucifixion
        fountains opened deep and wide;
     through the floodgates of God's mercy
        flowed a vast and gracious tide.
     Grace and love, like mighty rivers,
        poured incessant from above,
     and heaven's peace and perfect justice
        kissed a guilty world in love.

                              WILLIAM REES (1802–1883)
                     translated by WILLIAM EDWARDS (1848–1929)

Music: ROBERT LOWRY (1826–1899)

1 How deep the Fa-ther's love for us, how vast be-yond all mea-

-sure, that he should give his on-ly Son to make a wretch his trea-

-sure. How great the pain of sear-ing loss; the Fa-ther turns his face a-

-way, as wounds which mar the cho-sen One bring ma-ny souls

to glo-ry.

Music: STUART TOWNEND (*b.* 1963)

1 How deep the Father's love for us,
   how vast beyond all measure,
   that he should give his only Son
   to make a wretch his treasure.
   How great the pain of searing loss;
   the Father turns his face away,
   as wounds which mar the chosen One
   bring many souls to glory.

2 Behold the man upon a cross,
   my sin upon his shoulders;
   ashamed, I hear my mocking voice
   call out among the scoffers.
   It was my sin that held him there,
   until it was accomplished;
   his dying breath has brought me life —
   I know that 'it is finished.'

3 I will not boast in anything,
   no gifts, no power, no wisdom;
   but I will boast in Jesus Christ,
   his death and resurrection.
   Why should I gain from his reward?
   I cannot give an answer;
   but this I know with all my heart,
   his wounds have paid my ransom.

STUART TOWNEND (b. 1963)

ONCE AGAIN

1 Je-sus Christ, I think up-on your sac-ri-fice; you be-came no - thing,

poured out to death. Ma-ny times I've wondered at your gift of life, and

I'm in that place_ once a-gain,_ I'm in that place_ once a-gain.

Refrain 𝄋 And once a-gain I look up-on the cross where you died,_ I'm

humbled by your mercy and I'm broken inside._ Once a-gain I thank you,

Fine (Optional)

once again I pour out my life._ 3 Thank you for the cross,

D.S. al Fine

thank you for the cross, thank you for the cross, my friend. friend. And

Music: MATT REDMAN (b. 1974)

1   Jesus Christ, I think upon your sacrifice;
       you became nothing, poured out to death.
    Many times I've wondered at your gift of life
       and I'm in that place once again,
       I'm in that place once again.

And once again I look upon
the cross where you died.
I'm humbled by your mercy
and I'm broken inside.
Once again I thank you,
once again I pour out my life.

2   Now you are exalted to the highest place,
       King of the heavens, where one day I'll bow.
    But for now I marvel at this saving grace
       and I'm full of praise once again,
       I'm full of praise once again.

And once again ...

* 3   Thank you for the cross,
    thank you for the cross,
       thank you for the cross, my friend.
    Thank you for the cross,
    thank you for the cross,
       thank you for the cross, my friend.

And once again ...

MATT REDMAN (*b.* 1974)

47   Words and Music: © 1995, Thankyou Music. Administered (UK and Europe) by kingswaysongs.com
<tym@kingsway.co.uk>. Remaining territories administered by worshiptogether.com songs. Used by permission.

AGINCOURT (DEO GRACIAS)   LM

1   See, Christ was wounded for our sake,
        and bruised and beaten for our sin,
    so by his sufferings we are healed,
        for God has laid our guilt on him.

2   Look on his face, come close to him —
        see, you will find no beauty there:
    despised, rejected, who can tell
        the grief and sorrow he must bear?

3   Like sheep that stray we leave God's path,
        to choose our own and not his will;
    like sheep to slaughter he has gone
        obedient to his Father's will.

4   Cast out to die by those he loved,
        reviled by those he died to save,
    see how sin's pride has sought his death,
        see how sin's hate has made his grave.

5   For on his shoulders God has laid
        the weight of sin that we should bear;
    so by his Passion we have peace,
        through his obedience and his prayer.

                        BRIAN FOLEY (1919–2000)
                        based on Isaiah 53

Music: English melody, 15th century, adapted
    arranged by DAVID ILIFF (b. 1939)

Refrain

Un - less a grain of wheat shall fall up - on the ground___ and die,___ it re - mains___ but a sin - gle grain___ with no life. _

To verses　　Last time

2 If

Cantor(s)

1 If we have died with him, then we shall live with him; if we hold firm we shall reign with him.___ Un -

2　If anyone serves me
　　then they must follow me;
　　wherever I am my servants will be.

3　Make your home in me
　　as I make mine in you;
　　those who remain in me bear much fruit.

4　If you remain in me
　　and my word lives in you,
　　then you will be my disciples.

5　Those who love me
　　are loved by my Father;
　　we shall be with them and dwell in them.

6　Peace I leave with you,
　　my peace I give to you;
　　peace which the world cannot give is my gift.

BERNADETTE FARRELL (b. 1957)
based on John 12

Music: BERNADETTE FARRELL (b. 1957)

WIDFORD

76 76 77 76

Music: JOHN BARNARD (b. 1948)

1 When you prayed beneath the trees,
  it was for me, O Lord;
 when you cried upon your knees,
  how could it be, O Lord?
 When in blood and sweat and tears
  you dismissed your final fears,
 when you faced the soldiers' spears,
  you stood for me, O Lord.

2 When their triumph looked complete,
  it was for me, O Lord;
 when it seemed like your defeat,
  they could not see, O Lord!
 When you faced the mob alone
  you were silent as a stone,
 and a tree became your throne;
  you came for me, O Lord.

3 When you stumbled up the road,
  you walked for me, O Lord,
 when you took your deadly load,
  that heavy tree, O Lord;
 when they lifted you on high
  and they nailed you up to die,
 and when darkness filled the sky,
  it was for me, O Lord.

4 When you spoke with kingly power,
  it was for me, O Lord;
 in that dread and destined hour,
  you made me free, O Lord;
 earth and heaven heard you shout,
  death and hell were put to rout,
 for the grave could not hold out;
  you are for me, O Lord.

CHRISTOPHER IDLE (b. 1938)

PALM SUNDAY

2   He comes the broken hearts to heal,
       the prisoners to free.
   The deaf shall hear, the lame shall dance,
       the blind shall see.

3   And those who mourn with heavy hearts,
       who weep and sigh,
   with laughter, joy and royal crown
       he'll beautify.

4   We call you now to worship him
       as Lord of all,
   to have no other gods but him:
       their thrones must fall!

GRAHAM KENDRICK   (*b.* 1950)

Music: GRAHAM KENDRICK (*b.* 1950)

SING HOSANNA

1 There's a man riding in on a donkey,_____ there's a
man, and they say he's king! And the palm leaves are waving a
welcome_____ and the voices of the people sing:

Descant
Sing ho-san-na, sing ho-san-na, sing ho-san-na

Refrain
Sing ho-san-na, sing ho-san-na, sing ho-san-na to the

to the King! Sing ho--san-na, sing ho--
King of kings! Sing ho-san-na, sing ho--

-san-na, sing ho--san-na to the King!
-san-na, sing ho-san-na to the King!

2   Why a king riding in on a donkey?
    Why a king wearing no fine crown?
    Where the drums, where the high-sounding cymbals
    if a king is riding into town?

3   Hear the voice of the King on a donkey!
    Hear the joy of the news he brings!
    He is Jesus, the Son of the Highest.
    He is Jesus and the King of kings.

PAUL WIGMORE (b.1925)

Music: arranged by JOHN BARNARD (b.1948)

You are the King of glo - ry, you are the Prince of

Peace, you are the Lord of heaven and earth,

you're the Son of right - eous - ness. An - gels fall down be -

fore___ you, wor - ship and a - dore, for you have the

words of e - ter - nal life,___ you are Je - sus Christ the Lord.

Ho - san - na to the Son of Da - vid! Ho - -

- san - na to the King of___ kings! Glo - ry in the

high - est hea - - ven for Je - sus the Mes - si - ah

Descant

reigns! Ho - san - na to the Son of Da - - vid! Ho -

Unison

Ho - san - na to the Son of Da - - vid! Ho -

- san - na to the King of kings! Glo - ry in the

- san - na to the King of___ kings! Glo - ry in the

high - est hea - - ven for Je - sus the Mes - si - ah reigns!

high - est hea - - ven for Je - sus the Mes - si - ah reigns!

You are the King of glory,
   you are the Prince of Peace,
you are the Lord of heaven and earth,
   you're the Son of righteousness.
Angels bow down before you,
   worship and adore,
for you have the words of eternal life,
   you are Jesus Christ the Lord.

Hosanna to the Son of David!
   Hosanna to the King of kings!
Glory in the highest heaven
   for Jesus the Messiah reigns!

Hosanna to the Son of David!
   Hosanna to the King of kings!
Glory in the highest heaven
   for Jesus the Messiah reigns!

MAVIS FORD

Music: MAVIS FORD
   arranged by JOHN BARNARD (b. 1948)

Music: South African
arranged by GEOFF WEAVER (b. 1943)

PALM SUNDAY

Sanna, sannanina,
sanna, sanna, sanna.
Sanna, sannanina,
sanna, sanna, sanna.

Sanna, sanna, sanna, sannanina,
sanna, sanna, sanna.
Sanna, sanna, sanna, sannanina,
sanna, sanna, sanna.

Derived from *Hosanna*

The song may be sung repeatedly in procession.

MAUNDY THURSDAY

BOW BRICKHILL   LM

For the blessing and reception of oils

1   Redeemer, Lord, your praise we sing
    and magnify your holy name;
    your gift of oil to you we bring,
    to us your saving power proclaim!

2   The sun in splendour warmed the ground
    that nourishes the olive tree;
    whose laden branches all around
    give oil for our infirmity.

3   So now this oil be richly blessed
    to us and all who feel its power,
    and may your name, in faith confessed,
    bring healing in a needful hour.

4   From those baptized, let Satan flee,
    his evil malice be undone;
    signed with the cross, the oil shall be
    a symbol of the war begun.

5   In every service, every task,
    may your anointing warm our soul,
    that by your Spirit, as we ask,
    the sign of oil shall make us whole.

* 6   Then let this time of vows renewed
    recall the Lord who died to save;
    and at his table, heaven's food
    proclaim his empty cross and grave.

MICHAEL SAWARD   (*b.*1932)

*The final verse may be sung at a Chrism Eucharist with
renewal of commitment to ministry.*

Music: SYDNEY HUGO NICHOLSON (1875–1947)

Refrain *Not too fast*

Faith, hope and love, these— three shall re-main, but the
great-est of all is love.

Cantor or All

1 Christ has gath-ered us to-ge-ther, filled our hearts with joy and
glad-ness. Let us love our God sin-cere-ly, lov-ing
one an-oth-er like-wise. God is tru-ly love.

2 Therefore when we are assembled,
banished be all sad divisions;
let all bitterness be ended,
strife and quarrels be forgotten
for the Lord is here.

3 Grant us, loving Lord, hereafter,
sight of your eternal glory,
joy with all the saints in heaven,
peace and happiness unbounded,
as we sing your praise.

STEPHEN DEAN (b. 1948)
based on *Ubi caritas* (Latin, 9th century)

Music: STEPHEN DEAN (b. 1948)

SURREY   88 88 88

Music: HENRY CAREY (1687–1743)

1   Great God, your love has called us here,
as we, by love, for love were made.
Your living likeness still we bear,
though marred, dishonoured, disobeyed.
   We come, with all our heart and mind
   your call to hear, your love to find.

2   We come with self-inflicted pains
of broken trust and chosen wrong,
half-free, half-bound by inner chains,
by social forces swept along,
   by powers and systems close confined,
   yet seeking hope for humankind.

3   Great God, in Christ you call our name
and then receive us as your own,
not through some merit, right or claim,
but by your gracious love alone.
   We strain to glimpse your mercy seat
   and find you kneeling at our feet.

4   Then take the towel, and break the bread,
and humble us, and call us friends.
Suffer and serve till all are fed,
and show how grandly love intends
   to work till all creation sings,
   to fill all worlds, to crown all things.

5   Great God, in Christ you set us free
your life to live, your joy to share.
Give us your Spirit's liberty
to turn from guilt and dull despair
   and offer all that faith can do,
   while love is making all things new.

BRIAN WREN (b. 1936)

57 Words: © 1975, 1995, Stainer & Bell Ltd, 23 Gruneisen Road, London N3 1DZ <www.stainer.co.uk>

SOUTHWELL   SM

Alternate verses may be sung by choir and congregation.

1   'Prepare a room for me,
             your Saviour, Host and Priest,
        where I may gather you, my friends,
             to celebrate the feast.'

2   'This room we have prepared;
             the Table now is set.
       We wait your promised presence, Lord,
             where we once more are met.'

3   'Where even two or three
             have come the Meal to share,
       unseen, but living, loving still,
             I surely will be there!'

4   'Lord Christ, we seek the food
             your grace alone can give.
       We come with empty, hungering hearts
             that we may eat and live.'

5   'My promise I will keep;
             your hunger will be fed,
       for in this meal I offer you
             myself, the living Bread!'

6   'All thanks and praise to you,
             our Saviour, Lord and Friend,
       that through this Loaf and Cup you share
             your love that has no end!'

                     HERMAN G. STUEMPFLE, JR   (1923–2007)

Music: Adapted from Psalm 45 in *The Psalmes in English Metre*, 1579
       arranged by WILLIAM DAMAN (1540–1591)

INTERCESSOR   II IO II IO

1   This is the night, dear friends, the night for weeping,
     when powers of darkness overcome the day,
     the night the faithful mourn the weight of evil
     whereby our sins the Son of Man betray.

2   This night the traitor, wolf within the sheepfold,
     betrays himself into his victim's will;
     the Lamb of God for sacrifice preparing,
     sin brings about the cure for sin's own ill.

3   This night Christ institutes his holy supper,
     blest food and drink for heart and soul and mind;
     this night injustice joins its hands to treason's,
     and buys the ransom-price of humankind.

4   This night the Lord by slaves shall be arrested,
     he who destroys our slavery to sin;
     accused of crime, to criminals be given,
     that judgement on the righteous Judge begin.

5   O make us sharers, Saviour, of your Passion,
     that we may share your glory that shall be;
     let us pass through these three dark nights of sorrow
     to Easter's laughter and its liberty.

Latin text by PETER ABÉLARD (1079–1142)
translated by RICHARD STURCH (*b.* 1936)

Music: CHARLES HUBERT HASTINGS PARRY (1848–1918)

SOMERSET   86 88 6

Music: arranged by DAVID ILIFF (*b.* 1939)
based on a Somerset folk song

1   Jesus, in dark Gethsemane,
       in anguish and dismay,
    keeping your watch alone, you weep
    with your disciples fast asleep.
       Keep us awake, we pray.

2   Your only consolation there —
       God's answer to your prayer —
    the strength to rise and make your way
    through deeper gloom to Calvary,
       to fathom our despair.

* 3   There, at your grief's extremity,
       in friendless agony,
    heaven descended into hell
    because in you God loved so well
       guilty humanity.

4   Now, through your tears and deep distress,
       your grief and loneliness,
    faith contemplates God's heart and knows
    the anguish love still undergoes,
       to heal our wretchedness.

5   When we must shoulder our own cross,
       Lord, join our will to yours;
    though flesh is weak, help us to cling
    to your nailed hands and, trusting, sing
       the triumph of your cause.

6   Keep us awake, Lord, strong in faith
       and let your Spirit's breath
    strengthen our voices in your praise
    through all time's hurtful, hopeful days,
       and through the void of death.

ALAN GAUNT (b. 1935)

60 Words: © 1991, Stainer & Bell Ltd, 23 Gruneisen Road, London N3 1DZ <www.stainer.co.uk>

(Continues on opposite page.)

Some or all of the optional verses, for one or more cantors, may be added once the ostinato has been sung at least twice.

Music: JACQUES BERTHIER (1923–1994)

MAUNDY THURSDAY

pray, watch and pray!

pray not to give way to temp - ta - tion.

but the flesh is weak.

pray,___ watch and pray.

- main here with me, stay a-wake and pray.

if it is pos-si-ble, let this cup pass me by.

drink-ing it, your will be done.

the Lord is com-ing!___

pray,___ watch and pray.___

* *Choose either part.*

Taizé Community
based on Matthew 26.36-42

GOOD FRIDAY

A PURPLE ROBE

1 A purple robe, a crown of thorn, a reed in his right
hand; before the soldiers' spite and scorn I
see my Saviour stand. 2 He bears between the
Roman guard the weight of all our woe; a
stumbling figure bowed and scarred I see my Saviour
go. 3 Fast to the cross's spreading span,
high in the sunlit air, all the unnumbered
sins of man I see my Saviour bear.

4 He hangs, by whom the world was made, beneath the darkened
sky; the everlasting ransom paid, I
see my Saviour die. 5 He shares on high his
Father's throne, who once in mercy came; for
all his love to sinners shown I sing my Saviour's
name.

TIMOTHY DUDLEY-SMITH (*b.* 1926)

Music: DAVID WILSON (*b.* 1940)
     arranged by NOËL TREDINNICK (*b.* 1949)

BRESLAU   LM

1   A time to watch, a time to pray,
      a day of wonders is today:
      the saddest, yet the gladdest too,
      that earth or heaven ever knew.

2   The saddest, for our Saviour bore
      his death, that we might die no more:
      the agony, the scourge, the fear,
      the crown of thorns, the cross, the spear.

3   And yet the gladdest, for today
      our load of sin was borne away:
      and hopes of joy that never dies
      hang on our Saviour's sacrifice.

4   O Saviour, how we bless your name!
      Yours is the glory, ours the shame;
      by all the pain your love endured
      let all our many sins be cured.

* JOHN MASON NEALE (1818–1866)

Music: German, 15th century, as adapted in *As hymnodus sacer,* Leipzig,
1625, *Probably harmonised by* WILLIAM HENRY MONK (1823–1889)

VEXILLA REGIS   LM

Unison

1 As roy - al ban - - - ners are____ un - furled,____
the cross dis - plays____ its my - - ste - - ry:____
the Ma - ker of___ our flesh,___ in flesh,___ im - paled_____ and
hang - - ing help - less - - ly.____ A - - men.____

Music: Mode i
     arranged by CHARLES CLEALL (*b.* 1927)

GOOD FRIDAY

1   As royal banners are unfurled,
        the cross displays its mystery:
    the Maker of our flesh, in flesh,
        impaled and hanging helplessly.

* 2   Already deeply wounded: see
        his side now riven by a spear,
    and all our sins are swept away
        by blood and water flowing here.

3   See everything the prophets wrote
        fulfilled in its totality,
    and tell the nations of the world
        our God is reigning from the tree.

* 4   This tree, ablaze with royal light
        and with the blood-red robe it wears,
    is hallowed and embellished by
        the weight of holiness it bears.

5   Stretched like a balance here, his arms
        have gauged the price of wickedness;
    but, hanging here, his love outweighs
        hell's unforgiving bitterness.

* 6   The Saviour, victim, sacrifice,
        is, through his dying, glorified;
    his life is overcome by death
        and leaps up, sweeping death aside.

7   We hail the cross, faith's one true hope:
        God's passion set in time and space,
    by which our guilt is blotted out,
        engulfed in such stupendous grace. Amen.

VENANTIUS FORTUNATUS (530–609)
translated by ALAN GAUNT (b. 1935)

1 Come and see, come and see, come and see the King of
2 (Come and) weep, come and mourn for your sin that pierced him
3 (Man of) heaven, born to earth to re-store us to your

love; see the pur-ple robe and crown of thorns he
there; so much deep-er than the wounds of thorn and
heaven, here we bow in awe be-neath your search-ing

wears._____ Sol-diers mock, ru-lers
nail._____ All our pride, all our
eyes._____ From your tears comes our

sneer, as he lifts the cru-el cross; lone and
greed, all our fall-en-ness and shame; and the
joy, from your death our life shall spring; by your

friend-less now he climbs to-wards the hill._____
Lord has laid the pu-nish-ment on him._____
re-sur-rec-tion pow-er we shall rise._____

Refrain

— We wor-ship at your feet, where

wrath and mer-cy meet, and a guil-ty world is

washed by love's pure stream._____ For us he was made

sin. Oh, help me take it in! Deep

GOOD FRIDAY

wounds of love cry out, 'Fa - ther, for - give!' _____ I

wor - - - ship, I wor - - - ship the

vv. 1,2   v. 3

Lamb_____ who was slain._____ 2 Come and __
                                   3 Man of

GRAHAM KENDRICK (b. 1950)

Music: GRAHAM KENDRICK (b. 1950)
arranged by CHRISTOPHER NORTON (b. 1953)

CAITHNESS

WALSALL

1 O cross of Christ, immortal tree
   on which our Saviour died,
   the world is sheltered by your arms
   that bore the Crucified.

2 From bitter death and barren wood
   the tree of life is made;
   its branches bear unfailing fruit
   and leaves that never fade.

3 O faithful cross, you stand unmoved
   while ages run their course:
   foundation of the universe,
   creation's binding force.

4 Give glory to the risen Christ
   and to his cross give praise,
   the sign of God's unfathomed love,
   the hope of all our days.

Stanbrook Abbey

Music: 1: Melody from *Scottish Psalter,* 1635
   harmonised by Compilers of *English Hymnal,* 1906

Music: 2: From William Anchors: *A Choice Collection of Psalm Tunes,* *c.* 1721
   harmonised by Compilers of *English Hymnal,* 1906

THE POWER OF THE CROSS

1 Oh, to see the dawn of the dark - est day:
Christ on the road to Cal - va - ry;

tried by sin - ful men, torn and beat - en, then
nailed to a cross of wood. ____

Refrain

This, the power____ of the cross:____ Christ be -
came____ sin for us;____ took the blame,____
bore the wrath: we stand for - giv - en at the cross.

2 Oh, to see the pain written on your face,
bearing the awesome weight of sin.
Every bitter thought, every evil deed
crowning your blood-stained brow.

3 Now the daylight flees, now the ground beneath
quakes as its Maker bows his head.
Curtain torn in two, dead are raised to life;
'Finished!' the victory cry.

4 Oh, to see my name written in the wounds,
for through your suffering I am free.
Death is crushed to death, life is mine to live,
won through your selfless love.

This the power of the cross:
Son of God — slain for us.
What a love! What a cost!
We stand forgiven at the cross.

KEITH GETTY (b. 1974)
and STUART TOWNEND (b. 1963)

Music: KEITH GETTY (b. 1974) and STUART TOWNEND (b. 1963)

PASSION CHORALE   76 76 D

1   This is your coronation —
        thorns pressed upon your head;
    no bright angelic heralds,
        but angry crowds instead;
    beneath your throne of timber,
        and struggling with the load,
    you go in cruel procession
        on sorrow's royal road.

2   Eternal judge on trial,
        God's law, by law denied;
    love's justice is rejected
        and truth is falsified.
    We who have charged, condemned you
        are sentenced by your love;
    your blood pronounces pardon
        as you are stretched above.

3   High Priest, you are anointed
        with blood upon your face,
    and in this hour appointed
        the offering for our race.
    For weakness interceding;
        for sin, you are the price;
    for us your prayer unceasing,
        O living sacrifice.

                    SYLVIA G. DUNSTAN (1955–1993)

Music: Traditional secular melody in Hans Leo Hassler's
        Lustgarten neuer teutscher Gesäng, 1601
        harmonised by JOHANN SEBASTIAN BACH (1685–1750)

HOLY SATURDAY

BOROUGH

1   Dark is the night, and friends lie sleeping still,
        and cold, Gethsemane, with dread and tears;
    lanterns and swords no radiance, no defence,
        bring to our Lord as pallid dawn appears.

2   Dark is the day, the temple veil is torn,
        and friends are hiding from his death and loss;
    a thief his love unfailing comes to know,
        the first-fruits of salvation by the cross.

3   Dark is the tomb, and friends stoop low to find
        if death has won indeed, or risen he;
    and we through doubting and despair with them
        prepare in faith his wondrous face to see.

PAUL WIGMORE (b. 1925)

Music: CYRIL TAYLOR (1907–1991)

GARSDALE HEAD   11 8 11 8

1   His cross stands empty in a world grown silent
      through hours of anguish and of dread;
  in stillness, earth awaits the resurrection,
      while Christ goes down to wake the dead.

2   He summons Adam and his generations,
      brings light where darkness endless seemed;
  he frees and claims his own, so long held captive,
      who with the living are redeemed.

3   With God the Father and the Holy Spirit,
      give praise to Christ the crucified,
  who through the ages seeks to save his lost ones:
      our sinful race for whom he died.

Stanbrook Abbey

Music: PETER MOGER (b. 1964)

EASTER VIGIL

Unison (Harmony (v. 2))

1   Exult, creation round God's throne!
      All heaven, rejoice! All angels, sing!
      Salvation's trumpet sound aloud
      for Jesus Christ, our risen King.

2   Exult, O earth, in radiant hope;
      in Christ's majestic splendour shine!
      The Lord is here, the victory won,
      the darkness drowned in light divine.

3   Exult, all Christians, one in praise
      with our Jerusalem above!
      This roof shall ring with Easter songs
      that echo Christ's redeeming love.

CHRISTOPHER IDLE *(b.* 1938)
based on *Exsultet jam angelica*
(The Easter Song of Praise)

Music: PAUL EDWARDS *(b.* 1955)

TYDDYN LLWYN   87 87 87 extended

Music: EVAN MORGAN (1846–1920)

1   I will sing the Lord's high triumph,
      ruling earth and sky and sea;
    God, my strength, my song, my glory,
      my salvation now is he.
    Through the waters, through the waters,
      God has brought us liberty,
      God has brought us liberty.

2   By the storm and at the mountain
      grace and judgement both are shown;
    all who planned his people's ruin
      power divine has overthrown.
    Nations tremble, nations tremble;
      God has made his mercy known,
      God has made his mercy known.

3   Who is like the God of Israel,
      faithful, holy, throned above?
    Stretching out the arm of anger,
      yet he guides us by his love.
    To our homeland, to our homeland,
      God will see us safely move,
      God will see us safely move.

4   Praise our God, who in the thunder
      led a nation through the sea;
    praise the One whose blood released us
      from our deeper slavery.
    Alleluia, alleluia,
      Christ is risen: we are free;
      Christ is risen: we are free!

CHRISTOPHER IDLE (b. 1938)
based on Exodus 15 (*The Song of Moses and Miriam*)

CHRIST BE OUR LIGHT

1 This is the night of new be - gin - nings. This is the night when hea - ven meets earth. This is the night filled with God's glo - ry, pro - mise of our new birth!

Descant

Christ, be our light! Shine out

Refrain

Christ, be our light! Shine in our hearts.

through the dark, shine! Christ,

Shine through the dark - - ness. Christ,

be our light! Shine in your church

be our light! Shine in your church

Music: BERNADETTE FARRELL (b. 1957)

ga - thered to - day.
_____

ga - thered to - day.
_____

1   This is the night of new beginnings.
    This is the night when heaven meets earth.
    This is the night filled with God's glory,
        promise of our new birth!

    Christ, be our light!
    Shine in our hearts. Shine through the darkness.
    Christ, be our light!
    Shine in your church gathered today.

2   This is the night Christ our Redeemer
    rose from the grave triumphant and free,
    leaving the tomb of evil and darkness
        empty for all to see.

3   Now will the fire kindled in darkness
    burn to dispel the shadows of night.
    Star of the morning, Jesus our Saviour,
        you are the world's true light!

4   Sing of the hope deeper than dying.
    Sing of the power stronger than death.
    Sing of the love endless as heaven,
        dawning throughout the earth.

5   Into this world morning is breaking;
    all of God's people, lift up your voice.
    Cry out with joy, tell out the story;
        all of the earth, rejoice!

BERNADETTE FARRELL (b. 1957)

peo - ple of Zi - on, sing__ for joy, for great in your midst,

D.C.

great in your midst is the Ho - ly One of Is - rael.__

We shall draw water joyfully,
singing joyfully, singing joyfully;
we shall draw water joyfully
from the wellsprings of salvation.

Cantor:
1 Truly God is our salvation;
we trust, we shall not fear.
For the Lord is our strength,
the Lord is our song;
he became our Saviour.

2 Give thanks, O give thanks to the Lord;
give praise to his holy name!
Make his mighty deeds known
to all of the nations;
proclaim his greatness.

3 Sing a psalm, sing a psalm to the Lord,
for he has done glorious deeds.
Make known his works to all of the earth;
people of Zion, sing for joy,
for great in your midst, great in your midst
is the Holy One of Israel.

PAUL INWOOD *(b. 1947)*
based on Isaiah 12.2-6 *(A Song of Deliverance)*

Music: PAUL INWOOD *(b. 1947)*

EASTER

1 All heaven de-clares   the glo-ry of the
ris - - en Lord.   Who can   com-pare
(v. 2) with the beau-ty of the Lord?   For-ev-er he will
be   the Lamb up-on__ the throne;
I glad-ly bow the knee   and wor-ship him a-lone.__

v. 1   v. 2

1   All heaven declares the glory of the risen Lord.
     Who can compare with the beauty of the Lord?
     Forever he will be the Lamb upon the throne;
      I gladly bow the knee and worship him alone.

2   I will proclaim the glory of the risen Lord,
     who once was slain to reconcile the world to God.
     Forever you will be the Lamb upon the throne;
      I gladly bow the knee and worship you alone.

NOEL RICHARDS (b. 1955)
and TRICIA RICHARDS (b. 1960)

Music: NOEL RICHARDS (b. 1955) and TRICIA RICHARDS (b. 1960)

EARTH AND ALL STARS   9 10 9 10 and refrain

Briskly

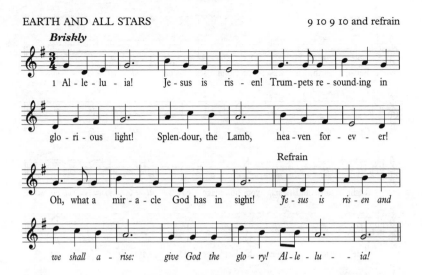

1 Al - le - lu - ia!   Je - sus is   ris - en!   Trum - pets re - sound-ing in

glo - ri - ous light!   Splen-dour, the   Lamb,   hea - ven for - ev - er!

Refrain

Oh, what a   mir - a - cle   God has in   sight!   *Je - sus is   ris - en and*

we shall a - rise: give God the   glo - ry!   Al - le - lu - - ia!

1 Alleluia! Jesus is risen!
  Trumpets resounding in glorious light!
  Splendour, the Lamb, heaven forever!
  Oh, what a miracle God has in sight!

  Jesus is risen and we shall arise:
  give God the glory! Alleluia!

2 Weeping, be gone; sorrow, be silent:
  death is defeated, and Easter is bright.
  Angels announce, 'Jesus is risen!'
  Clothe us in wonder, adorn us in light.

3 Walking the way, Christ walking with us,
  telling the story to open our eyes;
  breaking the bread, showing his glory;
  Jesus our blessing, our constant surprise.

     HERBERT F. BROKERING (1926–2009)

Music: DAVID N. JOHNSON (1922–1987)

STUEMPFLE   LM and Alleluias

1 Earth, earth, a-wake; your prai-ses sing: *Al - le - lu - ia!*

Greet with the dawn your ri-sen King: *Al - le - lu - ia!*

Bright suns and stars, your ho-mage pay: *Al - le - lu - - ia!*____

Life reigns a-gain this Eas-ter Day: *Al - le - lu - ia!*

1   Earth, earth, awake; your praises sing: Alleluia!
       Greet with the dawn your risen King: Alleluia!
       Bright suns and stars, your homage pay: Alleluia!
       Life reigns again this Easter Day: Alleluia!

2   All nature sings of hope reborn: Alleluia!
       Christ lives to comfort those who mourn: Alleluia!
       First fruit of all the dead who sleep: Alleluia!
       Promise of joy for all who weep: Alleluia!

3   Winter is past, the night is gone: Alleluia!
       Christ's light, triumphant, pales the dawn: Alleluia!
       Creation spreads its springtime bloom: Alleluia!
       Life bursts like flame from death's cold tomb: Alleluia!

4   Praise we the Father, Spirit, Son: Alleluia!
       Praise we the victory God has won: Alleluia!
       Praise we the Lamb who reigns above: Alleluia!
       Praise we the King whose rule is love: Alleluia!

HERMAN G. STUEMPFLE, JR   (1923–2007)

Music: SALLY ANN MORRIS (b. 1952)

KINGSFOLD   DCM

1   If Christ had not been raised from death
       our faith would be in vain,
    our preaching but a waste of breath,
       our sin and guilt remain.
    But now the Lord is risen indeed;
       he rules in earth and heaven:
    his gospel meets a world of need —
       in Christ we are forgiven.

2   If Christ still lay within the tomb
       then death would be the end,
    and we should face our final doom
       with neither guide nor friend.
    But now the Saviour is raised up,
       so when a Christian dies
    we mourn, yet look to God in hope —
       in Christ the saints arise!

3   If Christ had not been truly raised
       his Church would live a lie;
    his name should nevermore be praised,
       his words deserve to die.
    But now our great Redeemer lives;
       through him we are restored:
    his word endures, his Church revives
       in Christ, our risen Lord.

CHRISTOPHER IDLE (*b.* 1938)
based on 1 Corinthians 15.12-20

Music: Melody from *English County Songs* 1893
harmonised by RALPH VAUGHAN WILLIAMS (1872–1958)

MFURAHINI HALELUYA   99 99 and refrain

1 Jesus is risen, alleluia! Worship and praise him, alleluia! Now our redeemer bursts from the grave: lost to the tomb, Christ rises to save. Come, let us worship him, endlessly sing; Christ is alive and death loses its sting. Sins are forgiven, alleluia! Jesus is risen, alleluia!

Music: Haya (Tanzanian) traditional melody
  arranged by JOHN L. BELL (b.1949)

79 Arrangement: From *Courage To Say No,* 1996. © 1996, Wild Goose Resource Group,
The Iona Community, 4th Floor, Savoy Centre, 140 Sauchiehall Street, Glasgow G2 3DH

1   Jesus is risen, alleluia!
    Worship and praise him, alleluia!
    Now our Redeemer bursts from the grave:
    lost to the tomb, Christ rises to save.

    Come, let us worship him, endlessly sing;
    Christ is alive and death loses its sting.
    Sins are forgiven, alleluia!
    Jesus is risen, alleluia!

2   Buried for three days, destined for death,
    now he returns to breathe with our breath.
    Blest are the ears alert to his voice,
    blest are the hearts which for him rejoice.

3   'Don't be afraid!' the angel had said,
    'Why seek the living here with the dead?
    Look, where he lay, his body is gone,
    risen and vibrant, warm with the sun.'

4   'Go and tell others, Christ is alive.'
    Love is eternal, faith and hope thrive.
    What God intended, Jesus fulfilled;
    what God conceives can never be killed.

5   Let heaven echo, let the earth sing:
    Jesus is saviour of everything.
    All those who trust him, Christ will receive;
    therefore rejoice, obey and believe!

                              BERNARD KYAMANYWA
              English version by JOHN L. BELL (b. 1949)

79   Words: From *Courage To Say No*, 1996. English version © 1996, Wild Goose Resource Group, The Iona Community, 4th Floor, Savoy Centre, 140 Sauchiehall Street, Glasgow G2 3DH

1 See, — what a morn - ing, glo - rious-ly bright, with the dawn - ing of
hope in Je - ru - sa-lem; fold - ed the grave-clothes, tomb — filled with
light, as the an - gels an-nounce Christ is ri - - sen!
See God's sal - va - tion— plan, wrought in love, borne in
pain,— paid in sac - ri-fice, ful - filled in
Christ, the— Man, for he lives: Christ is ri - sen from the

vv. 1,2   *Last time*

dead!—

2   See Mary weeping, 'Where is he laid?'
    as in sorrow she turns from the empty tomb;
    hears a voice speaking, calling her name;
    it's the Master, the Lord raised to life again!
        The voice that spans the years,
    speaking life, stirring hope, bringing peace to us,
        will sound till he appears,
    for he lives: Christ is risen from the dead!

3   One with the Father, Ancient of Days,
    through the Spirit who clothes faith with certainty;
    honour and blessing, glory and praise
    to the King crowned with power and authority!
        And we are raised with him,
    death is dead, love has won, Christ has conquered;
        and we shall reign with him,
    for he lives: Christ is risen from the dead!

STUART TOWNEND (b. 1963) and KEITH GETTY (b. 1974)

Music: STUART TOWNEND (b. 1963) and KEITH GETTY (b. 1974)

NOEL NOUVELET   11 11 10 11

1   Word that formed creation, earth and sea and sky;
      Word that brings salvation, Word that will not die;
    speak now in us that we might hear your call;
      Living Word of Jesus, sound within us all.

2   Love that formed and named us, filled this clay with breath;
      Love that seeks and claims us, Love beyond all death;
    come now and fire the life that flows from you;
      Love that raised up Jesus, raise us up anew.

3   Song of joy and wonder, sound so wild and free;
      voice of wind and thunder, boundless as the sea;
    Music of God, the love that casts out fear;
      Song that sang in Jesus, sing within us here.

4   God of all creation, form our hearts anew;
      God of our salvation, lead us home to you;
    Spirit, inspire our hearts to hear your call;
      living God of Jesus, come renew us all!

                                        MARTY HAUGEN (b. 1950)

Music: French carol, 15th century
    harmonised by DAVID ILIFF (b. 1939)

CHRISTCHURCH   66 66 88

1 You shall go out with joy
 and come again in peace;
 the mountains and the hills
 shall sing and never cease;
 the Son of God is ris'n again,
 his love has conquered death's domain.

2 The trees in every field
 shall clap their hands, and say
 'Come shout aloud, and help
 us celebrate this day!'
 Jesus, the King, has burst the grave,
 and lives once more to heal and save.

3 The Word, like rain or snow,
 has come down from above,
 and now reveals to all
 God's purposes of love;
 the Word made flesh, once dead, now lives,
 new life to all he freely gives.

4 The myrtle for the briar,
 the cypress for the thorn,
 shall rise to tell the world
 of its awaking dawn.
 Jesus, the Life, the Truth, the Way,
 has ushered in God's great new day.

N. T. WRIGHT (b. 1948)
based on Isaiah 55.10-13

Music: CHARLES STEGGALL (1826–1905)

CELTIC ALLELUIA

Al - - le - lu - - ia, al - le - - lu - - ia. Al - le - -

Al - - le - lu - - ia, al - le - - lu - - ia. Al - - le -

- lu - - ia, al - le - - lu - - ia.

- lu - - ia, al - le - - lu - - - ia.

Cantor or Choir

Now he is liv- ing, the Christ. Out of the tomb he is

ris - en; he has con - quered death,__ o - pened

hea - ven to all be - - liev - ers. ____

FINTAN O'CARROLL (1922–1981)
and CHRISTOPHER WALKER (b. 1947)

Music: FINTAN O'CARROLL (1922–1981) and CHRISTOPHER WALKER (b. 1947)

ASCENSION DAY

CHRISTCHURCH   66 66 44 44

1   Ascended Christ, who gained
    the glory that we sing,
    anointed and ordained,
    our Prophet, Priest and King:
        by many tongues
        the Church displays
        your power and praise
        in all her songs.

2   No titles, thrones, or powers
    can ever rival yours;
    no passing mood of ours
    can turn aside your laws:
        you reign above
        each other name
        of worth or fame,
        the Lord of love!

Music: CHARLES STEGGALL (1826–1905)

3   Now from your Father's side
you make your people new;
since for our sins you died
our lives belong to you:
    from our distress
    you set us free
    for purity
    and holiness.

4   You call us to belong
within one body here;
in weakness we are strong
and all your gifts we share:
    in you alone
    we are complete
    and at your feet
    with joy bow down.

5   All strength is in your hand,
all power to you is given;
all wisdom to command
in earth and hell and heaven:
    beyond all words
    creation sings
    the King of kings
    and Lord of lords.

CHRISTOPHER IDLE (b. 1938)

MARIUS

1   Clap your hands all you nations,
        Amen. Hallelujah!
     shout for joy all you people;
        Amen. Hallelujah!
     Holy is the Most High;
        Amen. Hallelujah!
     mighty over the earth.
        Amen. Hallelujah!

2   God subdues every nation,
     God is king of all creatures;
     God has given this land,
     to the people he loves.

3   To the shouting in triumph,
     to the blasting of trumpets,
     God has gone up,
     God ascends over all.

4   Praise the Lord with your singing,
     sing God psalms for ever.
     God is monarch of all,
     sovereign over the earth.

5   Those on earth who are mighty
     still belong to our Maker,
     God exalted on high,
     God for ever our Lord.

JOHN L. BELL (b. 1949)
based on Psalm 47

Music: JOHN L. BELL (b. 1949)

85   Words and Music: From *Psalms of Patience, Protest & Praise,* 1993. © 1993, Wild Goose Resource Group,
The Iona Community, 4th Floor, Savoy Centre, 140 Sauchiehall Street, Glasgow G2 3DH

BARNARD GATE   11 10 11 10

1   Come, see the Lord in his breathtaking splendour:
      gaze at his majesty — bow and adore!
      Enter his presence with wonder and worship —
      he is the King, and enthroned evermore.

2   He is the Word who was sent by the Father,
      born as a baby, a child of our race:
      God here among us, revealed as a servant,
      walking the pathway of truth and of grace.

3   He is the Lamb who was slain to redeem us —
      there at the cross his appearance was marred;
      though he emerged from the grave as a victor,
      still from the nails and the spear he is scarred.

4   He is the Lord who ascended in triumph —
      ever the sound of his praises shall ring!
      Hail him the First and the Last, the Almighty:
      Jesus, our Prophet, our Priest and our King.

5   Come, see the Lord in his breathtaking splendour:
      gaze at his majesty — bow and adore!
      Come and acknowledge him Saviour and Sovereign:
      Jesus our King is enthroned evermore.

MARTIN LECKEBUSCH (*b.* 1962)

Music: JOHN BARNARD (*b.* 1948)

COLBOOTH   10 10 10 and Alleluia

1 Ho - ly for - ev - er and ev - er is God,

o - ver all crea - tures the so - ve - reign Lord,

who was, and is, and who is yet to come. Al - le -

- lu - - - ia!

A - - - men.

Music: JOHN L. BELL (*b.* 1949)

1   Holy forever and ever is God,
over all creatures the sovereign Lord,
who was, and is, and who is yet to come.
   Alleluia!

2   Praise to our Maker and Mover we sing,
glory and honour and blessing we bring;
all our existence depends on the Lord.
   Alleluia!

3   Worthy are you who, by shedding your blood,
brought from all nations a people for God.
Folk of all races you call to be priests.
   Alleluia!

4   Worthy the Lamb who was sentenced and slain!
Worthy the Lamb in his rising again!
Worthy of power and wisdom and wealth,
   alleluia!

5   Blessing and honour and glory and might
be to the Lamb on the throne, as is right.
Let earth and heaven unite to exclaim
   alleluia! Amen.

JOHN L. BELL (b. 1949)
based on Revelation 5, 7

87 Words and Music: From *Enemy of Apathy*, 1988. © 1988, Wild Goose Resource Group,
The Iona Community, 4th Floor, Savoy Centre, 140 Sauchiehall Street, Glasgow G2 3DH

ASCENSION to PENTECOST

ORIENTIS PARTIBUS   77 77 and Alleluia

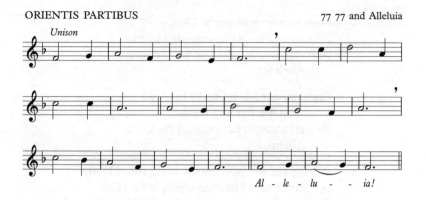

Al - le - lu - - - ia!

Music: French mediæval melody
harmonised by RALPH VAUGHAN WILLIAMS (1872–1958)

1   All together in one place
        friends of Jesus met to pray,
    waiting as the Lord had said
        for the Pentecostal day.
        Alleluia!

2   All together with one power
        poured out when the Spirit came,
    touching each and filling all,
        rushing wind and burning flame.
        Alleluia!

3   All together with one voice,
        praising God in every tongue:
    languages they never learned,
        telling what the Lord had done.
        Alleluia!

4   All together with one aim:
        bearing witness to their Lord —
    sharing faith by word and deed,
        preaching Christ, the living Word.
        Alleluia!

5   All together still today,
        though two thousand years have gone.
    Still the Spirit's power is given;
        still God's people meet as one.
        Alleluia!

6   One in mission, one in faith,
        still responding to God's call,
    one in telling all the world
        Jesus Christ is Lord of all!
        Alleluia!

BRIAN HOARE (*b.* 1935)

REPTON   86 886 extended

1   Be present, Spirit of the Lord,
      let sounds of earth be dumb;
      the Father's love be shed abroad,
      the dew of blessing on us poured:
         O silent Spirit, come!
         O silent Spirit, come!

2   In power unseen upon us rest,
      your gracious gifts impart:
      a mind renewed, a spirit blessed,
      a life where Christ is manifest,
         an understanding heart,
         an understanding heart.

3   Love's sovereign work of grace fulfil,
      our souls to Christ incline,
      intent to do the Father's will
      and stand by faith before him still
         in righteousness divine,
         in righteousness divine.

4   O Spirit come, and with us stay;
      make every heart your home.
      So work in us that we who pray
      may walk with Christ in wisdom's way:
         O Holy Spirit, come!
         O Holy Spirit, come!

                  TIMOTHY DUDLEY-SMITH (*b.* 1926)

Music: CHARLES HUBERT HASTINGS PARRY (1848–1918)
      from the oratorio *Judith*

YR HUN GÂN   87 87 D

1   Holy Spirit, gift bestower,
       breathe into our hearts today.
    Flowing water, dove that hovers,
       Holy Spirit, guide our way.
    Love inspirer, joy releaser,
       Spirit, take our fears away.
    Reconciler, peace restorer,
       move among us while we pray.

2   Holy Spirit, Christ proclaimer,
       wisdom bringer, light our way.
    Fire that dances, wind that whispers,
       Holy Spirit, come today.
    Ease disturber, comfort bearer,
       move among us while we pray.
    Truth revealer, faith confirmer,
       rest within our hearts today.

Author unknown

Music: Welsh traditional melody
       arranged by Compilers of *Church Hymnary,* 4th edition, 2005

GLENFINLAS   65 65

1   Holy Spirit, hear us;
       help us while we sing;
    breathe into the music
       of the praise we bring.

2   Holy Spirit, prompt us
       when we try to pray;
    nearer come, and teach us
       what we ought to say.

3   Holy Spirit, teach us
       through the words we read;
    bring to life the Bible
       with the light we need.

4   Holy Spirit, give us
       each a lively mind;
    make us more like Jesus,
       gracious, pure and kind.

5   Holy Spirit, help us
       daily, by your might,
    what is wrong to conquer,
       and to choose the right.

                * WILLIAM HENRY PARKER (1845–1929)

Music: KENNETH GEORGE FINLAY (1882–1974)
    harmonised by the composer for *Methodist Hymnbook,* 1933.

BRIDEGROOM   87 87 6

Unison

1   Like the murmur of the dove's song,
       like the challenge of her flight,
    like the vigour of the wind's rush,
       like the new flame's eager might:
       come, Holy Spirit, come.

2   To the members of Christ's Body,
       to the branches of the Vine,
    to the Church in faith assembled,
       to her midst as gift and sign:
       come, Holy Spirit, come.

3   With the healing of division,
       with the ceaseless voice of prayer,
    with the power to love and witness,
       with the peace beyond compare:
       come, Holy Spirit, come.

CARL P. DAW, JR (*b.* 1944)

Music: PETER CUTTS (*b.* 1937)

LAVENDON

10 10 10 10

1   May we, O Holy Spirit, bear your fruit —
      your joy and peace pervade each word we say;
    may love become of life the very root,
      and grow more deep and strong with every day.

2   May patience stem the harmful word and deed,
      and kindness seek the good among the wrong;
    may goodness far beyond our lips proceed,
      as manifest in action as in song.

3   May faithfulness endure, yet as we grow
      may gentleness lend courage to the weak;
    and in our self-restraint help us to know
      the grace that made the King of Heaven meek.

PAUL WIGMORE (*b.* 1925)

Music: PAUL EDWARDS (*b.* 1955)

THAINAKY

1 She sits like a bird, brood-ing on the wa-ters, hover-ing on the cha-os of the world's first day: she sighs and she sings, mo-ther-ing cre-a-tion, wait-ing to give birth to all the Word will say.

2   She wings over earth,
      resting where she wishes,
   lighting close at hand or soaring through the skies;
      she nests in the womb,
      welcoming each wonder,
   nourishing potential hidden to our eyes.

3   She dances in fire,
      startling her spectators,
   waking tongues of ecstasy where dumbness reigned;
      she weans and inspires
      all whose hearts are open,
   nor can she be captured, silenced, or restrained.

4   For she is the Spirit,
      one with God in essence,
   gifted by the Saviour in eternal love;
      and she is the key
      opening the Scriptures,
   enemy of apathy and heavenly dove.

JOHN L. BELL (b.1949)
and GRAHAM MAULE (b.1958)

Music: JOHN L. BELL (b.1949)

94 Words and Music: From *Enemy of Apathy,* 1988. © 1988, Wild Goose Resource Group,
The Iona Community, 4th Floor, Savoy Centre, 140 Sauchiehall Street, Glasgow G2 3DH

BLOW THE WIND SOUTHERLY   13 10 13 10 and refrain

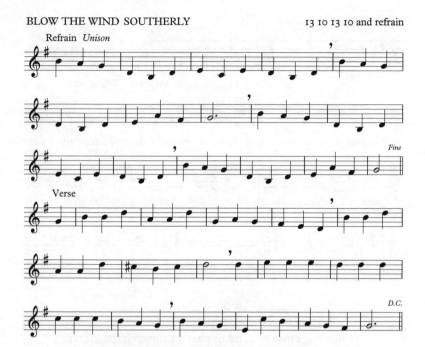

Spirit of holiness, wisdom and faithfulness,
Wind of the Lord, blowing strongly and free:
strength of our serving and joy of our worshipping —
Spirit of God, bring your fulness to me!

1   You came to interpret and teach us effectively
     all that the Saviour has spoken and done;
     to glorify Jesus is all your activity —
     promise and gift of the Father and Son:

2   You came with your gifts to supply all our poverty,
     pouring your love on the Church in her need;
     you came with your fruit for our growth to maturity,
     richly refreshing the souls that you feed:

3   You came to the world in its pride and futility,
     warning of dangers, directing us home;
     now with us and in us, we welcome your company;
     Spirit of Christ, in his name you have come:

                                CHRISTOPHER IDLE (b. 1938)

Music: English traditional melody
       arranged by JOHN BARNARD (b. 1948)

BREATH OF HEAVEN

Come, Ho - ly Spi - - rit, de - scend on us, de -

- scend on us; we ga - ther here in Je - - sus'

vv. 1 - 8

Cantor(s): 1 Come, _ Ho - ly Spi - rit.

Last time

name. (Hum) _____ Come, Ho - ly name. _____

Come, Holy Spirit,
descend on us, descend on us;
we gather here in Jesus' name.

Cantor:

1 Come, Holy Spirit.

2 Come, Breath of Heaven.

3 Come, Word of Mercy.

4 Come, Fire of Judgement.

5 Come, Great Creator.

6 Come to unite us.

7 Come to disturb us.

8 Come to inspire us.

JOHN L. BELL (*b.*1949)

Music: JOHN L. BELL (*b.*1949)

96 Words and Music: From *Come All You People*, 1995. © 1995, Wild Goose Resource Group,
The Iona Community, 4th Floor, Savoy Centre, 140 Sauchiehall Street, Glasgow G2 3DH

Cantor(s)

1 Come, Ho — ly Spi – rit of God.

2 Send forth your light and your truth.

3 Ho — ly Spi – rit make___ us one.___

Ostinato

Je – sus is Lord.___ Al – le – lu – ia!___

Come, re — new the face of the earth.

Guide us with your pow – er – ful love.

Al – le – lu – ia, al – le – lu – ia!

Je – sus is Lord.___ Al – le – lu – ia!

The melody of the Ostinato is first sung by the Cantor. One or more verses may be sung above the Ostinato, alternating with the Ostinato alone.

Music: JAMES WALSH (b. 1940)

Jesus is Lord. Alleluia!
Jesus is Lord. Alleluia!

Cantor:

1 Come, Holy Spirit of God.
 Come, renew the face of the earth.

2 Send forth your light and your truth.
 Guide us with your powerful love.

3 Holy Spirit, make us one.
 Alleluia, alleluia!

JAMES WALSH (*b.*1940)

98

Spi - rit of the liv - ing God, fall a-fresh on me;

Spi - rit of the liv - ing God, fall a-fresh on me;

break me, melt me, mould me, fill me;

Spi - rit of the liv - ing God, fall a-fresh on me.

DANIEL IVERSON (1890–1977)

Music: DANIEL IVERSON (1890–1977)
 arranged by PETER MOGER (*b.*1964)

The verses may be sung by one or more cantors above the ostinato refrain.

Veni, veni,
veni, veni,
veni Sancte Spiritus.
Veni, veni,
veni, veni,
Sancte Spiritus.

(Come, Holy Spirit.)

Cantor:

1 Come, make our hearts your home,
give us grace, Spirit, come.

2 Come, come thou well of life,
come thou fire of love.

3 Come, fill our hearts with heavenly love,
come, strengthen from above.

4 Come, keep us all from danger free,
come, peace that dwells in thee.

PETER NARDONE (*b.* 1965)

Music: PETER NARDONE (*b.* 1965)

Ostinato

Ve - - ni   Sanc - - te   Spi - - ri - - tus,
Ho - - ly   Spi - - rit,   come   to   us,

tu - i a - mo - ris   i - gnem ac - cen - de.   Ve - ni   Sanc - te
kin - dle in us   the   fire   of your love. ___   Ho - ly   Spi - rit,

Spi - - ri - tus,   ve - ni   Sanc - te   Spi - - ri - tus.
come   to   us,   Ho - ly   Spi - rit,   come _ to   us.

The verses may be sung by one or more cantors above the ostinato refrain.

> *Veni Sancte Spiritus,*
> *tui amoris ignem accende.*
> *Veni Sancte Spiritus,*
> *veni Sancte Spiritus.*
>
> *[English alternative:*
> *Holy Spirit, come to us,*
> *kindle in us the fire of your love.*
> *Holy Spirit, come to us,*
> *Holy Spirit, come to us.]*

Taizé Community
verses from John 13, 15, 1 John 3, 4

Music: JACQUES BERTHIER (1923–1994)

Cantor(s)

1 Je-sus said, 'I give you a new com-mand-ment:
Love one an - oth - er just as I have loved you.'

2 Je-sus said, 'It is by your love for one an-oth - er,
that ev-ery-one will re-cog-nize you as my di - sci - ples.'

3 Je-sus said, 'No one has great-er love than this:
to lay down one's life for those one loves.'

4 We
know love by this, that Christ laid down his life for us.

5 This is love:
it is not we who have loved God but God who loved us.

6 God is love, and those who a -
bide in love a - bide in God and God in them.

Choose either part.

TRINITY SUNDAY

ST MATTHEW

DCM

Music: A Supplement to the New Version, 1708
probably by WILLIAM CROFT (1678–1727)

1   Affirm anew the three-fold name
      of Father, Spirit, Son,
    our God whose saving acts proclaim
      a world's salvation won.
    In him alone we live and move
      and breath and being find,
    the wayward children of his love
      who cares for humankind.

2   Declare in all the earth his grace,
      to every heart his call,
    the living Lord of time and place
      whose love embraces all.
    So shall his endless praise be sung,
      his teaching truly heard,
    and every culture, every tongue,
      receive his timeless word.

3   Confirm our faith in this our day
      amid earth's shifting sand,
    with Christ as Life and Truth and Way,
      a Rock on which to stand;
    the one eternal Son and Lord
      by God the Father given,
    the true and life-imparting Word,
      the Way that leads to heaven.

4   Renew once more the ancient fire,
      let love our hearts inflame;
    renew, restore, unite, inspire
      the Church that bears your name;
    one name exalted over all,
      one Father, Spirit, Son,
    O grant us grace to heed your call
      and in that name be one.

TIMOTHY DUDLEY-SMITH (b. 1926)

WILBY   888 10 10

1 Christ pours his
2 God's changeless
3 Come, Spi - rit,

grace up - on his   own,   and where the word of life is
love shall nev - er   fail.   Though pow'rs of sin and death as -
then and make us   one.   Ful - fil your work of grace be -

sown   there shall the fruits of grace be   grown:
- - sail,   his pur - pose stands and shall pre - vail,
- - gun: and now as Fa - ther, Spi - rit, Son,

to him be glo - - ry,   whose cross and Pas - sion have
to him be glo - - ry,   our great Cre - a - tor, e -
to God be glo - - ry   from us his child - ren, through -

vv. 1,2

bought and saved us;   to__ him be glo - - ry.
- ter - nal Fa - ther,   to__ him be glo - - ry.
- out all ag - es,   to__ God be glo - -

v. 3

- ry.   To God be glo - ry   from us his child - ren, through -

- out all a - ges,   to__ God be glo - - ry.

Music: ANNE HARRISON (b. 1954)

1   Christ pours his grace upon his own,
     and where the word of life is sown
     there shall the fruit of grace be grown:
        to him be glory, whose cross and Passion
        have bought and saved us; to him be glory.

2   God's changeless love shall never fail.
     Though powers of sin and death assail,
     his purpose stands and shall prevail:
        to him be glory, our great Creator,
        eternal Father, to him be glory.

3   Come, Spirit, then and make us one.
     Fulfil your work of grace begun:
     and now as Father, Spirit, Son,
        to God be glory from us his children,
        throughout all ages, to God be glory.
        To God be glory from us his children,
        throughout all ages, to God be glory.

TIMOTHY DUDLEY-SMITH (b. 1926)

STUTTGART   87 87

1   Father, Lord of earth and heaven,
       King to whom all gifts belong,
    give your greatest gift, your Spirit,
       God the holy, God the strong.

2   Son of God, enthroned in glory,
       send your promised gift of grace;
    make your Church your holy temple,
       God the Spirit's dwelling-place.

3   Spirit, come in peace descending
       as at Jordan, heavenly dove;
    seal your Church as God's anointed,
       set our hearts on fire with love.

4   Stay among us, God the Father,
       stay among us, God the Son,
    stay among us, Holy Spirit:
       dwell within us, make us one.

                    JAMES QUINN, SJ   (1919–2010)

Music: Adapted from a melody in *Psalmodia Sacra*, Gotha, 1715
    possibly by CHRISTIAN FRIEDRICH WITT (*c.* 1660–1716)

HURST GREEN   10 10 4 4 10

1   Father, Lord! We give you adoration,
      who, through the gift of life, yourself have given.
        Hold us in light,
        keep clear our sight,
      give us the vision of your glorious way.

2   Jesus, Son! You taught by your example,
      that we on earth should live to sing your love.
        Teach us to pray,
        help us to stay
      close to the way which you to us have shown.

3   Spirit, God! You came to the disciples,
      filled them with love and light for all to see.
        Keep us aware,
        through love and care,
      you are the way by which we live our lives.

4   Holy Three! and greater than the heavens,
      power overwhelming, greater than the earth.
        Save us through love,
        and, from above,
      your way will prove to us the life of love.

PETER NARDONE (b. 1965)

Music: PETER NARDONE (b. 1965)

RANDOLPH   77 77

Harmony

Unison

1 Holy, holy, holy One,
   Love's eternal Trinity;
  we who hear your call, respond:
   'Here I am, my God, send me.'

2 Holy Source of all that lives,
   through creation's mystery,
  your love speaks and we reply,
   'Here I am, my God, send me.'

3 Holy Lamb, Love's sacrifice,
   mighty in humility,
  overawed we humbly say,
   'Here I am, my God, send me.'

4 Holy Spirit, Deathless Joy,
   though we face Love's agony,
  touch our lips and we will cry,
   'Here I am, my God, send me.'

5 Three times holy, loving God,
   call our name, and we will be
  each Love's living sacrifice:
   Here I am, my God, send me!

ALAN GAUNT (*b.*1935)

Music: RALPH VAUGHAN WILLIAMS (1872–1958)

THE TRANSFIGURATION of our LORD

ST ALBINUS · 78 78 and Alleluia

Al - le - lu - ia!

1. Jesus, on the mountain peak,
   stands alone in glory blazing.
   Let us, if we dare to speak,
   join the saints and angels praising:
   Alleluia!

2. Trembling at his feet we saw
   Moses and Elijah speaking.
   All the Prophets and the Law
   shout through them their joyful greeting:
   Alleluia!

3. Swift the cloud of glory came,
   God, proclaiming in its thunder,
   Jesus as his Son by name!
   Nations, cry aloud in wonder:
   Alleluia!

4. Jesus is the chosen One,
   living hope of every nation;
   hear and heed him, everyone;
   sing, with earth and all creation,
   Alleluia!

BRIAN WREN (*b.* 1936)

Music: HENRY JOHN GAUNTLETT (1805–1876)

1 Je - sus, re - store to us a - gain the gos - pel of your ho - ly name, that comes with power, not words a - lone, owned, signed and sealed from hea - ven's throne. Spi - rit and word in one a - greed; the pro - mise to the pow - er wed.

Refrain

The word is near, here in our mouths and in our hearts, the word of faith; pro - claim it on the Spi - rit's breath: Je - - - - - - sus!

Music: GRAHAM KENDRICK (b. 1950)

1   Jesus, restore to us again
the gospel of your holy name,
that comes with power, not words alone,
owned, signed and sealed from heaven's throne.
Spirit and word in one agreed;
the promise to the power wed.

The word is near, here in our mouths
and in our hearts, the word of faith:
proclaim it on the Spirit's breath: Jesus!

2   Your word, O Lord, eternal stands,
fixed and unchanging in the heavens.
The Word made flesh, to earth come down
to heal our world with nail-pierced hands.
Among us here you lived and breathed,
you are the message we received.

3   Spirit of truth, lead us, we pray
into all truth as we obey.
And as God's will we gladly choose,
your ancient powers again will prove
Christ's teaching truly comes from God,
he is indeed the living Word.

4   Upon the heights of this great land
with Moses and Elijah stand.
Reveal your glory once again,
show us your face, declare your name.
Prophets and Law, in you complete
where promises and power meet.

5   Grant us in this decisive hour
to know the Scriptures and the power:
the knowledge in experience proved,
the power that moves and works by love.
May word and works join hands as one,
the word go forth, the Spirit come.

GRAHAM KENDRICK (b. 1950)

107 Words and Music: © 1992, Graham Kendrick / Make Way Music Ltd, PO Box 320,
Tunbridge Wells, Kent. TN2 9DE UK. <www.grahamkendrick.co.uk> Used by permission.

SHINE, JESUS, SHINE

1 Lord, the light of your love is shin - ing,
2 Lord, I come to your awe - some pre - sence,
3 As we gaze on your king - ly bright - ness

in the midst of the dark - ness, shin - ing: Je - sus, Light of the
from the sha - dows in - to your ra - diance; by the blood I may
so our fa - ces dis - play your like - ness, ev - er chang - ing from

world, shine up - on us; set us free by the truth you now bring us,
en - ter your bright - ness: search me, try me, con - sume all my dark - ness:
glo - ry to glo - ry: mir - rored here, may our lives tell your sto - ry:

shine on me, shine on me.

Refrain

Shine, Je - sus, shine, fill this land with the Fa - ther's
glo - ry; blaze, Spi - rit, blaze, set our hearts on
fire. Flow, ri - ver, flow, flood the
na - - tions with grace and mer - cy; send forth your word,

vv. 1,2 | *v. 3*

Lord, and let there be light! light!

TRANSFIGURATION

1 Lord, the light of your love is shining,
 in the midst of the darkness shining:
 Jesus, Light of the world, shine upon us;
 set us free by the truth you now bring us:
 shine on me, shine on me.

 Shine, Jesus, shine,
 fill this land with the Father's glory;
 blaze, Spirit, blaze,
 set our hearts on fire.
 Flow, river, flow,
 flood the nations with grace and mercy;
 send forth your word, Lord,
 and let there be light!

2 Lord, I come to your awesome presence,
 from the shadows into your radiance;
 by the blood I may enter your brightness:
 search me, try me, consume all my darkness:
 shine on me, shine on me.

3 As we gaze on your kingly brightness
 so our faces display your likeness,
 ever changing from glory to glory:
 mirrored here, may our lives tell your story:
 shine on me, shine on me.

GRAHAM KENDRICK (b. 1950)

Music: GRAHAM KENDRICK (b. 1950)
 arranged by DAVID ILIFF (b. 1939)

HARVEST THANKSGIVING

REGENT SQUARE   87 87 87

Music: HENRY THOMAS SMART (1813–1879)
descant and v. 4 arrangement by JOHN BARNARD (b. 1948)

1 Fill your hearts with joy and gladness,
  sing and praise your God and mine!
 Great the Lord in love and wisdom,
  might and majesty divine!
 He who framed the starry heavens
  knows and names them as they shine.

2 Praise the Lord, his people, praise him!
  Wounded souls his comfort know;
 those who fear him find his mercies,
  peace for pain and joy for woe;
 humble hearts are high exalted,
  human pride and power laid low.

3 Praise the Lord for times and seasons,
  cloud and sunshine, wind and rain;
 spring to melt the snows of winter
  till the waters flow again;
 grass upon the mountain pastures,
  golden valleys thick with grain.

4 Fill your hearts with joy and gladness,
  peace and plenty crown your days;
 love his laws, declare his judgements,
  walk in all his words and ways;
 he the Lord and we his children:
  praise the Lord, all people, praise!

TIMOTHY DUDLEY-SMITH (b. 1926)
based on Psalm 147

EAST ACKLAM   84 84 8884

1   For the fruits of all creation,
        thanks be to God;
     for the gifts to every nation,
        thanks be to God;
     for the ploughing, sowing, reaping,
     silent growth while we are sleeping,
     future needs in earth's safe-keeping,
        thanks be to God.

2   In the just reward of labour,
        God's will is done;
     in the help we give our neighbour,
        God's will is done;
     in our world-wide task of caring
     for the hungry and despairing,
     in the harvests we are sharing,
        God's will is done.

3   For the harvests of the Spirit,
        thanks be to God;
     for the good we all inherit,
        thanks be to God;
     for the wonders that astound us,
     for the truths that still confound us,
     most of all, that love has found us,
        thanks be to God.

FRED PRATT GREEN (1903–2000)

Music: FRANCIS JACKSON (b. 1917)

MADRID   67 67 and refrain

1 Praise God for har-vest-time, sing tell bells of hea-ven chime!
Sing of his love re-vealed, fruit of earth and o-cean's yield:

Refrain

Al - - le - - lu - - ia!   Al - - le - - lu - - ia!

Good har-vest safe-ly stored: praise our great Cre - a - tor Lord!

2   Plough turning soil and stone
by the winter stormwinds blown;
green buds on bending bough,
life to bring us harvest now:

3   God in the fertile land
joining with our human hand;
seed waking in the earth
stirring at the spring of birth:

4   See in our food a sign
pointing to a love divine;
strength from a summer sky,
life bestowed as rainclouds fly:

5   Lord, on your gifts we feed:
show us each the other's need;
give us the love to share
in our deeds and in our prayer:

6   Lord, from your plenteous field
land and sea their harvest yield;
these, Lord, we bring to you,
gifts that by your goodness grew:

PAUL WIGMORE (b. 1925)

Music: Melody anonymous, Philadelphia, 1824
arranged by JOHN BARNARD (b. 1948)

DEDICATION FESTIVAL

1 I re - joiced when I heard them say: 'Let us go to the house of God.' And now our feet are stand - ing in your gates, O Je - ru - sa - lem!

Refrain

Sha - lom, sha - lom, the peace of God be here. Sha - lom, sha - lom, God's jus - tice be ev - er near.

vv. 1 - 4   *Last time*

2 Like a near.

Music: BERNADETTE FARRELL (b. 1957)

1   I rejoiced when I heard them say:
'Let us go to the house of God.'
And now our feet are standing
in your gates, O Jerusalem!

Shalom, shalom, the peace of God be here.
Shalom, shalom, God's justice be ever near.

2   Like a temple of unity
is the city, Jerusalem.
It is there all tribes will gather,
all the tribes of the house of God.

3   It is faithful to Israel's law,
there to praise the name of God.
All the judgement seats of David
were set down in Jerusalem.

4   For the peace of all nations, pray:
for God's peace within your homes.
May God's lasting peace surround us;
may it dwell in Jerusalem.

5   For the love of my friends and kin
I will bless you with signs of peace.
For the love of God's own people
I will labour and pray for you.

BERNADETTE FARRELL (b. 1957)
based on Psalm 122

ABBOT'S LEIGH

87 87 D

Music: CYRIL TAYLOR (1907–1991)

1 Lord of all your love's creation,
present in each time and place,
may this earthly house of worship
be a source of heavenly grace.
Spirit, who at Christ's baptizing
came upon him as a dove,
come, renew for us that symbol,
seal us in God's faith and love.

2 Word of God, made flesh in Jesus,
help us read, mark, learn and feed
on your written word of power,
reaching to our every need.
For the preaching of the gospel,
making known your word to all,
Lord, we pray, and for the preachers
humbly answering your call.

* 3 When we meet around your table,
Lord, be here in bread and wine,
real to us who find your presence
in the world as in this sign.
Christ, whose cross is foolish wisdom,
teach us sacrificial ways
to reveal your truth to strangers,
welcome them in pilgrims' praise.

4 Praise to God whose power within us
helps us more than we can say,
in the church, and in Christ Jesus,
in each age, and day by day.
So we join in common worship,
sharing in this house of prayer;
come, Lord God, among your people:
may all say that 'God is there!'

STEPHEN PARISH (b. 1949)

SAINTS

WELLS HOUSE

Unison

LM

O WALY WALY

LM

1   For all the saints who showed your love
in how they lived and where they moved,
for mindful women, caring men,
accept our gratitude again.

2   For all the saints who loved your name,
whose faith increased the Saviour's fame,
who sang your songs and shared your word,
accept our gratitude, good Lord.

3   For all the saints who named your will,
and saw your kingdom coming still
through selfless protest, prayer and praise,
accept the gratitude we raise.

4   Bless all whose will or name or love
reflects the grace of heaven above.
Though unacclaimed by earthly powers,
your life through theirs has hallowed ours.

JOHN L. BELL (*b.* 1949)
and GRAHAM MAULE (*b.* 1958)

Music: 1: DAVID ILIFF (*b.* 1939)
Music: 2: English traditional melody
    arranged by NOËL TREDINNICK (*b.* 1949)

LOVE UNKNOWN 66 66 44 44

Unison

1   Glory to you, O God,
    for all your saints in light,
    who nobly waged and won
    the fierce and well-fought fight.
        Their praises sing,
        who life outpoured
        by fire and sword
        for Christ their King.

2   Thanks be to you, O Lord,
    for saints your Spirit stirred
    in humble paths to live
    your life and speak your word.
        Unnumbered they
        whose shining light
        informs our sight
        from day to day.

3   Lord God of truth and love,
    'Your kingdom come', we pray;
    give us your grace to know
    your truth and walk your way.
        Your will be done
        here on this earth,
        till saints in earth
        and heaven are one.

* HOWARD CHARLES ADIE GAUNT (1902–1983)

Music: JOHN NICHOLSON IRELAND (1879–1962)

OLD 104th   10 10 11 11

1   Rejoice in God's saints, today and all days!
     A world without saints forgets how to praise.
        Their faith in acquiring the habit of prayer,
        their depth of adoring, Lord, help us to share.

2   Some march with events to turn them God's way;
     some need to withdraw, the better to pray;
        some carry the gospel through fire and through flood:
        our world is their parish, their purpose is God.

3   Rejoice in those saints, unpraised and unknown,
     who bear someone's cross or shoulder their own:
        they shame our complaining, our comforts, our cares:
        what patience in caring, what courage, is theirs!

4   Rejoice in God's saints, today and all days!
     A world without saints forgets how to praise.
        In loving, in living, they prove it is true:
        the way of self-giving, Lord, leads us to you.

                                    FRED PRATT GREEN (1903–2000)

Music: Melody in Ravenscroft's *Psalmes,* 1621
     harmonised by RALPH VAUGHAN WILLIAMS (1872–1958)

LOBE DEN HERREN   14 14 4 7 8

1   Thanks be to God for his saints of each past generation,
     one with us still in one body, one great congregation;
            with them proclaim
            Jesus for ever the same,
            Author of life and salvation.

2   Thanks be to God for his blessings which daily surround us;
     glory to Christ, the Redeemer who sought us and found us,
            who from the grave
            rose, the almighty to save,
            breaking the fetters that bound us.

3   Thanks be to God for the years that are yet in his keeping,
     trusting each day to the care of a Father unsleeping,
            on to the end,
            Christ our companion and friend,
            joy at the last for our weeping.

4   Thanks be to God who has called us and daily defends us,
     who with the Son and the Spirit unchanging befriends us;
            now in that name,
            Jesus for ever the same,
            forth to his service he sends us.

                              TIMOTHY DUDLEY-SMITH (b. 1926)

Music: German 17th-century melody
       harmonised by Editors of *The Chorale Book for England*, 1863

CHRISTIAN INITIATION

LONG LANE   87 87

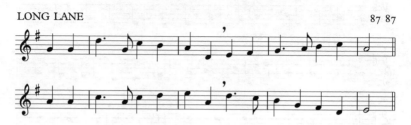

1   At the dawning of creation
        when the world began to be,
    God called forth the world's foundations
        from the deep chaotic sea.

2   When the Lord delivered Israel
        out of Egypt's bitter yoke,
    then the parting of the waters
        of the living water spoke.

3   Water from the rock of Moses,
        water from the temple's side,
    water from the heart of Jesus,
        flow in this baptismal tide.

4   Thus united in this water
        each to all, and each to Christ;
    to his life of love he calls us
        by his total sacrifice.

DAVID FOX (1956–2008)

Music: PETER NARDONE (*b.* 1965)

MORNING HYMN   LM

The second tune, DEUS TUORUM MILITUM, *is found overleaf.*

1   Awake, awake: fling off the night!
        For God has sent his glorious light;
     and we who live in Christ's new day
        must works of darkness put away.

2   Awake and rise, with love renewed,
        and with the Spirit's power endued.
     The light of life in us must glow,
        and fruits of truth and goodness show.

3   Let in the light: all sin expose
        to Christ, whose life no darkness knows.
     Before his cross for guidance kneel;
        his light will judge and, judging, heal.

4   Awake, and rise up from the dead,
        and Christ his light on you will shed.
     Its power will wrong desires destroy,
        and your whole nature fill with joy.

5   Then sing for joy, and use each day;
        give thanks for everything alway.
     Lift up your hearts; with one accord
        praise God through Jesus Christ our Lord.

                    JOHN RAPHAEL PEACEY (1896–1971)

Music: Melody by FRANÇOIS HYPPOLYTE BARTHÉLÉMON (1741–1808)

DEUS TUORUM MILITUM   LM

1   Awake, awake: fling off the night!
        For God has sent his glorious light;
     and we who live in Christ's new day
        must works of darkness put away.

2   Awake and rise, with love renewed,
        and with the Spirit's power endued.
     The light of life in us must glow,
        and fruits of truth and goodness show.

3   Let in the light: all sin expose
        to Christ, whose life no darkness knows.
     Before his cross for guidance kneel;
        his light will judge and, judging, heal.

4   Awake, and rise up from the dead,
        and Christ his light on you will shed.
     Its power will wrong desires destroy,
        and your whole nature fill with joy.

5   Then sing for joy, and use each day;
        give thanks for everything alway.
     Lift up your hearts; with one accord
        praise God through Jesus Christ our Lord.

JOHN RAPHAEL PEACEY (1896–1971)

Music: Grenoble church melody
    harmonised by MICHAEL FLEMING (1928–2006)

SHIPSTON   87 87

1   Child of blessing, child of promise,
    God's you are, from God you came.
    In this sacrament God claims you:
    live as one who bears Christ's name.

2   Child of God, you bear God's image;
    learn to listen for God's call;
    grow to laugh and sing and worship,
    trust and love God more than all.

RONALD S. COLE-TURNER (*b.* 1948)

Music: Melody from *English County Songs* 1893
    harmonised by RALPH VAUGHAN WILLIAMS (1872–1958)

Refrain

Do not be a-fraid,_____ for I have re-deemed you.____

_ I have called you by your name;_____ you are mine.____

_ 1 When you walk through the wa-ters, I'll be
2 When the fire is burn-ing all a-
3 When the fear of lone-li-ness is
4 When you dwell in the ex-ile of the
5 You are mine, O my child; I am your

with you. You will nev-er sink be-neath_ the_ waves.
round you, you will nev-er be con-sumed_ by the flames.
loom-ing, then re-mem-ber I am at_ your_ side.
stran-ger, re-mem-ber you are pre-cious in my eyes.
Fa-ther, and I love you with a per--fect_ love.

GERARD MARKLAND (b. 1953)
based on Isaiah 43.1-4

Music: GERARD MARKLAND (b. 1953)
arranged by ANNE HARRISON (b. 1954)

ANDERSON

7775

Unison

1 Freed in Christ from death and sin,
slaves no more to self within,
let abundant life begin
 at the call of Christ.

2 Out of darkness into light,
given grace to walk aright,
strength and courage for the fight,
 turned to follow Christ.

3 In the Spirit's life to grow,
day by day his fullness know,
and in fruitful lives to show
 we belong to Christ.

4 Bearers of his name and sign,
sharers in his bread and wine,
one with him in life divine,
 keeping faith with Christ.

5 Praise him for his love outpoured,
lives renewed and hopes restored;
praise the everlasting Lord,
 glory be to Christ!

TIMOTHY DUDLEY-SMITH (*b.* 1926)

Music: JANE MARSHALL (*b.* 1924)

BLAENWERN   87 87 D

Music: WILLIAM PENFRO ROWLANDS (1860–1937)

1   Source and fount of all creation,
       pour your Spirit from above
    on the bearers of your image,
    offspring of a human love.
    Human hopes and human graces
       break beneath the weight of sin;
    fear and envy wrench asunder
    world without and self within.

2   Human love is unavailing
       counter-weight to sin and strife;
    love of God alone can hold us
    on the way that leads to life.
    Praised be God, whose Son our Saviour
       human nature has restored,
    living, dying, raised in glory,
    to the likeness of its Lord.

3   Trace, O Christ, salvation's pattern,
    God and sinner reconciled,
    in an all-embracing story:
    new creation, new-born child.
    Word incarnate, world's Redeemer,
       here in us your work repeat,
    signed and sealed your own for ever,
    till the pattern stands complete.

4   Christ our universal Saviour,
       nature's poet, nature's priest,
    through life's troubled waters bring us
    to the eucharistic feast,
    where rejoicing saint and sinner
       praise the Lord of time and space,
    Father, Son and Holy Spirit,
    fount of being, source of grace.

PETER BAELZ (1923–2000)

Water of life,

cleanse and re-fresh us; raise us to life in Christ Je - - sus.

Cantor(s) or All

1 All you who thirst, come to the wa - - - ters,

and you will ne - ver be thir - sty a - gain.

Water of life, cleanse and refresh us;
raise us to life in Christ Jesus.

1   All you who thirst, come to the waters;
and you will never be thirsty again.

2   As rain from heaven, so is God's word,
it waters the earth and brings forth life.

3   Dying with Christ, so we shall rise with him,
death shall no longer have power over us.

4   Turn to the Lord, cast off your wickedness,
you will find peace in his infinite love.

STEPHEN DEAN (b. 1948)

Music: STEPHEN DEAN (b. 1948)

LEONI   66 84 D

1   We turn to Christ anew
       who hear his call today,
    his way to walk, his will pursue,
       his word obey.
    To serve him as our King
       and of his kingdom learn,
    from sin and every evil thing
       to him we turn.

2   We trust in Christ to save;
       in him new life begins:
    who by his cross a ransom gave
       from all our sins.
    Our spirits' strength and stay
       who when all flesh is dust
    will keep us on that final day,
       in him we trust.

3   We would be true to him
       till earthly journeys end,
    whose love no passing years can dim,
       our changeless friend.
    May we who bear his name
       our faith and love renew,
    to follow Christ our single aim,
       and find him true.

                          TIMOTHY DUDLEY-SMITH (b. 1926)

Music: Hebrew melody *noted by* THOMAS OLIVERS (1725–1799)

WORD OF GOD   87 87

1 Word of God, re- -new your peo- -ple, make us
now your liv-ing sign. Re-cre-ate us for your
pur-pose in this place and in this time.

2   Word of hope and Word of healing,
        make us now your living sign.
        Recreate us for your purpose
        in this place and in this time.

3   Word of peace and Word of justice,
        make us now your living sign.
        Recreate us for your purpose
        in this place and in this time.

4   God alone the power we trust in,
        make us now your living sign.
        Recreate us for your purpose
        in this place and in this time.

* 5   To the waters lead your people,
        make us now your living sign.
        Recreate us for your purpose
        in this place and in this time.

BERNADETTE FARRELL   (b. 1957)

*The final verse is suitable for the renewal of baptismal
promises in Epiphany or during the Easter Vigil.
Without the final verse, the song is also suitable for Lent.*

Music: BERNADETTE FARRELL (b. 1957)

May be sung in procession to the font.

Refrain

As the deer longs for run-ning streams, so I long, so I long, so I long for you.

1 A-thirst my soul for you, the God who is my life! When shall I see,

2 E-choes ...

(Optional sung or hummed accompaniment v. 3)

As the deer longs for run-ning streams, so I long,

when shall I see, see the face of God?

so I long, so I long for you.

2   Echoes meet as deep is calling unto deep,
      over my head, all your mighty waters,
        sweeping over me.

3   Continually the foe delights in taunting me:
      'Where is God, where is your God?'
        Where, oh where are you?

4   Defend me, God; send forth your light and your truth.
      They will lead me to your holy mountain,
        to your dwelling place.

5   Then shall I go unto the altar of my God.
      Praising you, O my joy and gladness,
        I shall praise your name.

BOB HURD *(b. 1950)*
based on Psalms 42, 43

Music: BOB HURD *(b. 1950)*
arranged by CRAIG KINGSBURY *(b. 1952)*

Turn over for music for verses 3 - 5.

May be sung in procession to the font.

In the Lord I'll be ever thankful,
in the Lord I will rejoice!
Look to God, do not be afraid.
Lift up your voices, the Lord is near;
lift up your voices, the Lord is near.

Cantor:

1   You are my salvation; I trust in you.
I shall not be afraid,
you are my strength; you are my song.

2   The Lord is my rock.
The Lord is my fortress.
My God, you are my refuge and my shield.

3   I call upon the Lord God who is worthy of praise.
The Lord shall save me.

4   My soul shall sing to you;
you have done wondrous things, O God.
Let this be known,
let this be known throughout the world.

5   With joy you will draw water at the fountain of salvation.
Give thanks to the Lord. Proclaim God's name.

Taizé Community
based on Isaiah 12.2-6 *(A Song of Deliverance)*, Psalm 18.2-3

Some or all of the optional verses, for one or more cantors, may be added once the ostinato has been sung at least twice.

Music: JACQUES BERTHIER (1923–1994)

3 I call up-on the Lord God who is wor-thy of

4 My soul shall sing to you;

5 With joy you will draw wa-ter at the foun-tain of sal-

Ostinato

In the Lord I'll be ev-er thank-ful, in the Lord I will re-

praise.

you have done won-drous things, O God. Let

-va-tion. Give thanks to the Lord.

-joice! Look to God, do not be a-fraid. Lift up your voi-ces, the

Behold, behold I make all things new,
beginning with you
and starting from today.
Behold, behold I make all things new,
my promise is true,
for I am Christ the Way.

JOHN L. BELL (b. 1949)
based on 2 Corinthians 5.17

Music: JOHN L. BELL (b. 1949)

Take, O take me as I am; sum-mon out what I shall be;

set your seal up-on my heart and live in me.

Take, O take me as I am;
summon out what I shall be;
set your seal upon my heart
and live in me.

JOHN L. BELL (b. 1949)

Music: JOHN L. BELL (b. 1949)

MARRIAGE

SUSSEX CAROL

88 88 88

Unison

1 As man and woman we were made
   that love be found and life begun:
the likeness of the living God,
   unique, yet called to live as one.
Through joy or sadness, calm or strife,
come, praise the love that gives us life.

2 Now Jesus lived and gave his love
   to make our life and loving new,
so celebrate with him today
   and drink the joy he offers you
that makes the simple moment shine
and changes water into wine.

3 And Jesus died to live again
   so praise the love that, come what may,
can bring the dawn and clear the skies,
   and waits to wipe all tears away;
and let us hope for what shall be
believing where we cannot see.

4 Then spread the table, clear the hall
   and celebrate till day is done;
let peace go deep between us all
   and joy be shared by everyone:
laugh and make merry with your friends
and praise the love that never ends!

BRIAN WREN (*b.*1936)

Music: English traditional melody
   arranged by RALPH VAUGHAN WILLIAMS (1872–1958)

WESTMINSTER ABBEY   87 87 87

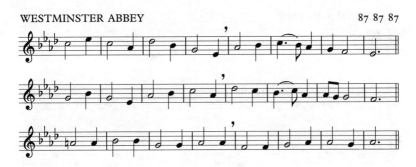

1   Lord and lover of creation,
      bless the marriage witnessed now:
    sign of lives no longer separate,
      sealed by symbol, bound by vow,
    celebrating love's commitment
      made to live and last and grow.

2   Praise and gratitude we offer,
      for the past which shaped today.
    Words which stirred and deepened conscience,
      family life, good company,
    friends who touched and summoned talent,
      nourished all words can't convey.

3   On your children wed and welcome
      here among us, we request
    health in home and hearts, and humour
      through which heaven and earth are blessed;
    open doors and human pleasure,
      time for touch and trust and rest.

4   Take them hence that, in each other,
      love fulfilling love shall find
    much to share and more to treasure,
      such that none dare break or bind
    those your name has joined together,
      one in body, heart and mind.

JOHN L. BELL (*b.*1949)
and GRAHAM MAULE (*b.*1958)

Music: HENRY PURCELL (1659–1695)
      arranged by ERNEST HAWKINS (1802–1868) *The Psalmist,* 1842

132 Words: From *Love From Below,* 1989. © 1989, Wild Goose Resource Group,
The Iona Community, 4th Floor, Savoy Centre, 140 Sauchiehall Street, Glasgow G2 3DH

STRENGTH AND STAY   11 10 11 10

1   Lord Jesus Christ, invited guest and saviour,
        with tender mercy hear us as we pray;
    grant our desire for those who seek your favour,
        come with your love and bless them both today.

2   Give them your strength for caring and for serving,
        give them your graces — faithfulness and prayer;
    make their resolve to follow you unswerving,
        make their reward your peace beyond compare.

3   Be their delight in joy, their hope in sorrow,
        be their true friend in pleasure as in pain;
    guest of today and guardian of tomorrow,
        turn humble water into wine again!

                                    MICHAEL PERRY (1942–1996)

Music: JOHN BACCHUS DYKES (1823–1876)

CONQUEST   86 86 88

1   Maker of all, whose word is life,
         inspire our human speech,
     as word of husband, word of wife,
         joins each in trust to each.
     Be with us, God of truth, to bless
     these promises of faithfulness.

2   Dear son of Mary, welcome guest,
         ready to take your share
     at Cana in a wedding feast
         and show your glory there,
     be with us, risen Christ, to bless
     this day of earthly happiness.

3   Spirit of goodness, grace and power,
         more close than thought or breath,
     whose guidance followed hour by hour
         makes sense of life and death,
     teach us in all our times of stress
     reliance on your steadfastness.

4   Trusting in you, your children ask
         for grace to keep their vow
     and share in your eternal task
         of loving here and now.
     May your sustaining presence bless
     two lives made one in faithfulness.

                    ELIZABETH J. COSNETT (b. 1936)

Music: DONALD S. BARROWS (1877–1951)

BRIDEGROOM   87 87 6

Unison

1   Not for tongues of heaven's angels,
       not for wisdom to discern,
       not for faith that masters mountains,
       for this better gift we yearn:
          may love be ours, O Lord.

2   Love is humble, love is gentle,
       love is tender, true and kind;
       love is gracious, ever patient,
       generous of heart and mind:
          may love be ours, O Lord.

3   Never jealous, never selfish,
       love will not rejoice in wrong;
       never boastful nor resentful,
       love believes and suffers long:
          may love be ours, O Lord.

4   In the day this world is fading
       faith and hope will play their part;
       but when Christ is seen in glory
       love shall reign in every heart:
          may love be ours, O Lord.

TIMOTHY DUDLEY-SMITH *(b. 1926)*
based on 1 Corinthians 13

Music: PETER CUTTS *(b. 1937)*

WHOLENESS and HEALING

DREAM ANGUS

Unison

1 Christ's is the world in which we move; Christ's are the
folk we're sum-moned to love; Christ's is the voice which
calls us to care, and Christ is the one who meets us here.

Refrain Harmony

To the lost Christ shows his face, to the un-loved he
gives his em-brace, to those who cry in pain or dis-
grace, Christ makes, with his friends, a touch-ing place.

2 Feel for the people we most avoid —
    strange or bereaved or never employed.
  Feel for the women and feel for the men
    who fear that their living is all in vain.

3 Feel for the parents who've lost their child,
    feel for the women whom men have defiled,
  feel for the baby for whom there's no breast,
    and feel for the weary who find no rest.

4 Feel for the lives by life confused,
    riddled with doubt, in loving abused;
  feel for the lonely heart, conscious of sin,
    which longs to be pure but fears to begin.

JOHN L. BELL *(b. 1949)*

and GRAHAM MAULE *(b. 1958)*

Music: Scottish folk melody
    harmonised by JOHN L. BELL *(b. 1949)*

136 Words: From *Love From Below*, 1989. © 1986, 1989, Wild Goose Resource Group,
The Iona Community, 4th Floor, Savoy Centre, 140 Sauchiehall Street, Glasgow G2 3DH

EBENEZER (TON-Y-BOTEL)

87 87 D

Music: THOMAS JOHN WILLIAMS (1869–1944)
adapted from an anthem

1 Jesus, in your life we see you
    making God's compassion known,
    'Surely you have borne our sorrows,
    surely made our pain your own!',
see your touch bring hope and healing,
    see your word set captives free,
see you suffer, mocked, rejected,
    dying on the shameful tree.

2 Risen Lord, you reign in glory;
    but your wounded hands still show
you can share the outcast's torment,
    sound the depths of human woe,
know where greed exploits the helpless,
    hear the addict's lonely cry,
grieve at so much waste and heartbreak,
    feel for all who question 'Why?'

3 Risen Lord, you bear their sorrow,
    know how much they need your peace;
as you once healed broken bodies,
    offered captive souls release,
take us, use us in your service;
    we would follow where you lead;
only your divine compassion
    meets the depths of human need.

BASIL BRIDGE (b. 1927)

137 Words: © 1999, Kevin Mayhew Ltd, Buxhall, Stowmarket, Suffolk IP14 3BW Used by permission.

SUSAN
87 87

1   Lay your healing hand upon us,
      Jesus, when we cry with pain;
   bind our wounds with your compassion;
      bring us back to health again.

2   Hold us like a gentle mother,
      heal the hurt we feel inside,
   set us on our feet and make us
      strong to take life in our stride.

3   With the confidence you give us,
      give us your compassion too,
   so that we may offer others
      comfort, healing, strength from you.

4   Then, whatever grief awaits us,
      as we learn your gentle ways
   we will share your joyful Spirit
      and for ever sing God's praise.

ALAN GAUNT (b. 1935)

Music: STEPHEN DEAN (b. 1948)

HOMEWARD   SM

SOUTHWELL   SM

1   Though hope desert my heart,
     though strangeness fill my soul,
    though truth torment my troubled mind,
     you have been here before.

2   Though confidence run dry,
     though weary flesh be sore,
    though conversation bear no fruit,
     you have been here before.

3   There is no threatening place,
     no trial I could know
    which has not known your presence first:
     you have been here before.

4   In Christ who, on the cross,
     felt all our hurt and more,
    and cried in deep abandonment,
     you have been here before.

5   I will not dread the dark,
     the fate beyond control,
    nor fear what reigns in frightening things:
     you will be there before.

JOHN L. BELL (*b.* 1949)

Music: 1: JOHN CROTHERS (*b.* 1948)
Music: 2: Adapted from Psalm 45 in *The Psalmes in English Metre*, 1579
    arranged by WILLIAM DAMAN (1540–1591)

YE BANKS AND BRAES (THE BANKS O' DOON) DLM

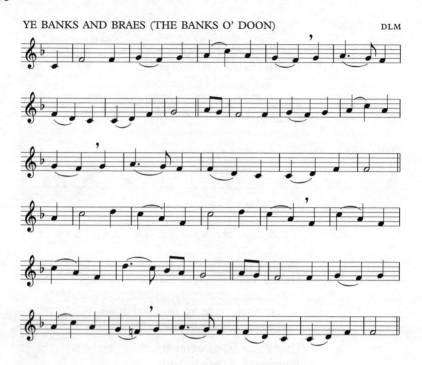

Music: Scottish folk melody
harmonised by JOHN L. BELL (*b.* 1949)

1   We cannot measure how you heal
or answer every sufferer's prayer,
yet we believe your grace responds
where faith and doubt unite to care.
Your hands, though bloodied on the cross,
survive to hold and heal and warn,
to carry all through death to life
and cradle children yet unborn.

2   The pain that will not go away,
the guilt that clings from things long past,
the fear of what the future holds
are present as if meant to last.
But present too is love which tends
the hurt we never hoped to find,
the private agonies inside,
the memories that haunt the mind.

3   So some have come who need your help
and some have come to make amends
as hands which shaped and saved the world
are present in the touch of friends.
Lord, let your Spirit meet us here
to mend the body, mind, and soul,
to disentangle peace from pain
and make your broken people whole.

JOHN L. BELL (b. 1949)
and GRAHAM MAULE (b. 1958)

140 Words: From *Love From Below*, 1989. © 1989, Wild Goose Resource Group, The Iona Community, 4th Floor, Savoy Centre, 140 Sauchiehall Street, Glasgow G2 3DH

CROSS DEEP   LM

1   We give God thanks for those who knew
        the touch of Jesus' healing love;
     they trusted him to make them whole,
        to give them peace, their guilt remove.

2   We offer prayer for all who go
        relying on God's grace and power,
     to help the anxious and the ill,
        to heal their wounds, their lives restore.

3   We dedicate our skills and time
        to those who suffer where we live,
     to bring such comfort as we can
        to meet their need, their pain relieve.

4   So Jesus' touch of healing grace
        lives on within our willing care;
     by thought and prayer and gifts we prove
        his mercy still, his love we share.

MICHAEL PERRY (1942–1996)

Music: BARRY ROSE (b. 1934)

Lord Jesus Christ, lover of all,
trail wide the hem of your garment.
Bring healing, bring peace.

JOHN L. BELL (*b.* 1949)
and GRAHAM MAULE (*b.* 1958)

May be sung as a response during intercessions, or before and after
a Bible reading, particularly at services of prayer for healing.

Music: PAUL STUBBINGS

143

ERISKAY LOVE LILT   77 66

2   Through the days of doubt and toil,
     in our joy and in our pain,
         guide our steps in your way,
         make us one in your love.

CATHERINE WALKER (*b.* 1958)

Music: Scottish folk melody
        arranged by Compilers of *Common Ground,* 1998

FUNERALS and the DEPARTED

WANLESS   10 10 10 10

1   Eternal God, supreme in tenderness,
      enfolding all creation in your grace;
        your mercy wraps us round, and ever shall,
        and in your purpose, all things shall be well.

2   Eternal Son, as one of us you came
      to be despised, made nothing, put to shame;
        and now, a mother comforting, you call,
        'All shall be well, and all things shall be well.'

3   Eternal Spirit, source of all delight,
      you stream in glory through the soul's dark night;
        we taste your spring of joy, for ever full,
        and know within that all things shall be well.

4   Eternal Trinity, through grief and pain,
      through all the malice by which love is slain,
        through all earth's anguish and the throes of hell,
        we trust to see, in you, all things made well.

ALAN GAUNT (b. 1935)
after Julian of Norwich

Music: JOHN HARPER (b. 1947)

WESSEX   11 10 11 10

1   Here from all nations, all tongues, and all peoples,
       countless the crowd but their voices are one;
       vast is the sight and majestic their singing:
       'God has the victory: he reigns from the throne!'

2   These have come out of the hardest oppression;
       now they may stand in the presence of God,
       serving their Lord day and night in his temple,
       ransomed and cleansed by the Lamb's precious blood.

3   Gone is their thirst and no more shall they hunger,
       God is their shelter, his power at their side:
       sun shall not pain them, no burning will torture;
       Jesus the Lamb is their shepherd and guide.

4   He will go with them to clear living water
       flowing from springs which his mercy supplies;
       gone is their grief and their trials are over,
       God wipes away every tear from their eyes.

5   Blessing and glory and wisdom and power
       be to the Saviour again and again;
       might and thanksgiving and honour for ever
       be to our God: Hallelujah! Amen.

CHRISTOPHER IDLE (*b.* 1938)
based on Revelation 7.9-17

Music: ALWYN SURPLICE (1906–1977)

OTTERY ST MARY   87 87

1   Lord, if faith is disenchanted,
        if our pain persists too long,
     show us that your love is planted
        deeper far than all time's wrong.

2   If we feel ourselves forsaken,
        overwhelmed by sin and grief,
     prove your love, though faith is shaken,
        deeper than our unbelief.

* 3   Where injustice and oppression
        make the poor and weak despair,
     prove your love's profound compassion,
        deeper than their deepest prayer.

* 4   When the children, Lord, are dying,
        anguished parents asking, 'Why?',
     prove your love, in grief and crying,
        deeper than grief's deepest cry.

5   Let the cross, your love's perfection,
        present with us all along,
     prove itself, in resurrection,
        deeper far than all time's wrong.

                                            ALAN GAUNT   (b. 1935)

Music: HENRY GEORGE LEY (1887–1962)

146   Words: © 1998, Stainer & Bell Ltd, 23 Gruneisen Road, London N3 1DZ <www.stainer.co.uk>
146   Music: © SPCK Publishing, 36 Causton Street, London SW1P 4ST, UK. Permission applied for.

JENNIFER

11 10 11 4

1 We can-not care for you the way we want-ed, or cra-dle you or
lis-ten for your cry; but, se-pa-ra-ted as we are by
si - lence, love will not die. breathes with your breath.

Following the death of a baby

1   We cannot care for you the way we wanted,
    or cradle you or listen for your cry;
    but, separated as we are by silence,
        love will not die.

2   We cannot watch you growing into childhood
    and find a new uniqueness every day;
    but special as you would have been among us,
        you still will stay.

3   We cannot know the pain or the potential
    which passing years would summon or reveal;
    but for that true fulfilment Jesus promised
        we hope and feel.

4   So through the mess of anger, grief and tiredness,
    through tensions which are not yet reconciled,
    we give to God the worship of our sorrow
        and our dear child.

5   Lord, in your arms, which cradle all creation
    we rest and place our baby beyond death,
    believing that *she / he* now, alive in heaven,
        breathes with your breath.

JOHN L. BELL (*b.* 1949)
and GRAHAM MAULE (*b.* 1958)

Music: JOHN L. BELL (*b.* 1949)

147   Words and Music: From *When Grief Is Raw*, 1996. © 1996, Wild Goose Resource Group,
The Iona Community, 4th Floor, Savoy Centre, 140 Sauchiehall Street, Glasgow G2 3DH

BARBARA ALLEN   87 87

1   When human voices cannot sing
        and human hearts are breaking,
    we bring our grief to you, O God
        who knows our inner aching.

2   Set free our spirits from all fear —
        the cloud of dark unknowing,
    and let the light, the Christ-light show
        the pathway of our going.

3   Make real for us your holding love,
        the love which is your meaning,
    the power to move the stone of death,
        the hope of Easter morning.

4   And let the one we love now go
        where we, in faith, shall follow,
    to travel in the Spirit's peace,
        to make an end to sorrow.

SHIRLEY ERENA MURRAY (b. 1931)

Music: English folk melody
    arranged by NOËL TREDINNICK (b. 1949)

149

UNDE ET MEMORES   10 10 10 10 10 10

For Remembrance Sunday

1   Eternal God, before whose face we stand,
your earthly children, fashioned by your hand,
hear and behold us, for to you alone
all hearts are open, all our longings known:
   so for our world and for ourselves we pray
   the gift of peace, O Lord, in this our day.

2   We come with grief, with thankfulness and pride,
to hold in honour those who served and died;
we bring our hurt, our loneliness and loss,
to him who hung forsaken on the cross;
   who, for our peace, our pains and sorrows bore,
   and with the Father lives for evermore.

3   O Prince of Peace, who gave for us your life,
look down in pity on our sin and strife.
May this remembrance move our hearts to build
a peace enduring, and a hope fulfilled,
   when every flag of tyranny is furled
   and wars at last shall cease in all the world.

4   From earth's long tale of suffering here below
we pray the fragile flower of peace may grow,
till cloud and darkness vanish from our skies
to see the Sun of Righteousness arise.
   When night is past and peace shall banish pain,
   all shall be well, in God's eternal reign.

TIMOTHY DUDLEY-SMITH (*b.* 1926)

Music: WILLIAM HENRY MONK (1823–1889)

150

THE CHURCH'S MINISTRY and MISSION

MEAD HOUSE   87 87 D

Music: CYRIL TAYLOR (1907–1991)

1   All-creating heavenly Giver,
       bringing light and life to birth;
    all-sustaining heavenly Father
       of the families of earth:
    we, your children, lift our voices
       singing gladly of your love:
    never-ending are the praises
       rising to your throne above.

2   Ever-living Lord and Saviour,
       breaking chains of sin and shame;
    ever-loving Intercessor,
       prayers are answered in your name:
    we, your servants, liberated
       at a fearsome ransom-price,
    in your kingdom are united
       by that mighty sacrifice.

3   Life-conceiving wind of heaven,
       breathing gifts upon us all;
    life-enhancing Spirit, given
       to enrich us, great and small:
    we, whose talents widely differ,
       now restore to you your own,
    and in true thanksgiving offer
       all we are before the throne.

4   Father, Son, and Holy Spirit,
       blessing all within your hand:
    full the cup that we inherit,
       firm the ground on which we stand:
    we, your people, undeserving
       of the grace you freely give,
    now and ever, in thanksgiving
       to your praise and glory live.

MICHAEL SAWARD (b. 1932)

LOVE UNKNOWN   66 66 44 44

1   Christ is the one who calls,
     the one who loved and came,
     to whom by right it falls
     to bear the highest name:
          and still today
          our hearts are stirred
          to hear his word
          and walk his way.

2   Christ is the one who seeks,
     to whom our souls are known.
     The word of love he speaks
     can wake a heart of stone;
          for at that sound
          the blind can see,
          the slave is free,
          the lost are found.

Music: JOHN NICHOLSON IRELAND (1879–1962)

3   Christ is the one who died
forsaken and betrayed;
who, mocked and crucified,
the price of pardon paid.
> Our dying Lord,
> what grief and loss,
> what bitter cross,
> our souls restored!

4   Christ is the one who rose
in glory from the grave,
to share his life with those
whom once he died to save.
> He drew death's sting
> and broke its chains,
> who lives and reigns,
> our risen King.

5   Christ is the one who sends,
his story to declare;
who calls his servants friends
and gives them news to share.
> His truth proclaim
> in all the earth,
> his matchless worth
> and saving name.

TIMOTHY DUDLEY-SMITH (b. 1926)

LUX EOI   87 87 D

Music: Arthur Seymour Sullivan (1842–1900)

1   Church of God, elect and glorious,
       holy nation, chosen race;
    called as God's own special people,
       royal priests and heirs of grace:
    know the purpose of your calling,
       show to all his mighty deeds;
    tell of love which knows no limits,
       grace which meets all human needs.

2   God has called you out of darkness
       into his most marvellous light;
    brought his truth to life within you,
       turned your blindness into sight.
    Let your light so shine around you
       that God's name is glorified;
    and all find fresh hope and purpose
       in Christ Jesus crucified.

3   Once you were an alien people,
       strangers to God's heart of love;
    but he brought you home in mercy,
       citizens of heaven above.
    Let his love flow out to others,
       let them feel a Father's care;
    that they too may know his welcome
       and his countless blessings share.

4   Church of God, elect and holy,
       be the people he intends;
    strong in faith and swift to answer
       each command your master sends:
    royal priests, fulfil your calling
       through your sacrifice and prayer;
    give your lives in joyful service —
       sing his praise, his love declare.

JAMES SEDDON   (1915–1983)

THE SERVANT KING

Not too fast

1 From heaven you came, help-less babe, en-tered our world, your glo-ry veiled; not to be served but to serve, and give your life that we might live. *This is our* **Refrain** *God,_____ the Ser-vant King,_____ he calls us now to fol-low him,_____ to bring our lives as a dai-ly of-fer-ing_____ of wor-ship to_____ the Servant King.*

Fine

D.C.

Music: GRAHAM KENDRICK (*b.* 1950)

1 From heaven you came, helpless babe,
   entered our world, your glory veiled;
   not to be served, but to serve,
   and give your life that we might live.

   This is our God, the Servant King,
   he calls us now to follow him,
   to bring our lives as a daily offering
   of worship to the Servant King.

2 There in the garden of tears,
   my heavy load he chose to bear;
   his heart with sorrow was torn,
   'Yet not my will but yours,' he said.

3 Come, see his hands and his feet,
   the scars that speak of sacrifice,
   hands that flung stars into space
   to cruel nails surrendered.

4 So let us learn how to serve,
   and in our lives enthrone him;
   each other's needs to prefer,
   for it is Christ we're serving.

GRAHAM KENDRICK (*b.* 1950)

GODMANCHESTER 10 10 10 10

6 Je - - sus, you call each one of us to serve:
a - - maz - ing grace we nev - er could de - serve.
Here we re - - new our de - di - ca - tion's vow:
Word of the Fa - ther, speak your sum - - mons now.

1 From the beginning, God's most holy Word
uttered the summons all creation heard;
Christ, the Word spoken, wisdom, power and light,
transforms the darkness of the deepest night,

2 Summons to wholeness all God's love enfolds,
cherishes, nurtures, gently shapes, remoulds
structures that fail, the institution's blight,
bathes disappointment in transforming light.

3 Jesus, the Word once spoken by the well,
challenges, heals as in response we tell
all our deep longings, all our hidden fears,
find then the solace of God's love and tears.

4 Lord, we are here your blessèd will to seek,
may each one listen to the word you speak.
Lord, be our succour as we work and pray,
give us fresh purpose this and every day.

5 Jesus, the Word once spoken by the tomb,
speak to our hearts in times of doubt and gloom.
Jesus the Word, our life, our hope, our breath,
draw us rejoicing from the sleep of death.

6 Jesus, you call each one of us to serve:
amazing grace we never could deserve.
Here we renew our dedication's vow:
Word of the Father, speak your summons now.

BRIGID PAILTHORPE (b. 1933)

Music: PETER MOGER (b. 1964)

HIGHWOOD

11 10 11 10

Music: RICHARD RUNCIMAN TERRY (1865–1938)

1   Glory to God, the source of all our mission;
    Jesus be praised, the Saviour, Lord and Son!
    Praise to the Spirit who confirms the vision;
    in all the world the will of God be done!

2   Proud in our wealth, or destitute and broken,
    we cannot live by earthly bread alone;
    but by the word that God himself has spoken
    we are set free to make our Master known.

3   Eastward or westward, northward, southward moving,
    finding new fields, new patterns and new role,
    Christ's fellow-workers, all his goodness proving,
    see how our God is making people whole!

4   Linked by the cross at which we are forgiven,
    joined by the love that came to find and save,
    one in the hope of God's new earth and heaven,
    we love and give since he first loved and gave.

5   Send us, Lord Christ, to serve at your direction,
    dying and living, yours in loss and gain,
    true to the gospel of your resurrection,
    working and praying till you come to reign.

CHRISTOPHER IDLE (*b.* 1938)

ENGELBERG   10 10 10 and Alleluia

1   Go to the world! Go into all the earth.
Go preach the cross where Christ renews life's worth,
baptizing as the sign of our rebirth.
Alleluia!

2   Go to the world! Go into every place.
Go live the Word of Christ's redeeming grace.
Go seek God's presence in each time and space.
Alleluia!

3   Go to the world! Go struggle, bless and pray;
the nights of tears give way to joyous day.
As servant Church, you follow Christ's own way.
Alleluia!

4   Go to the world! Go as the ones I send,
for I am with you till the age shall end,
when all the hosts of glory cry 'Amen!'
Alleluia!

SYLVIA G. DUNSTAN (1955–1993)

Music: CHARLES VILLIERS STANFORD (1852–1924)
arranged by Compilers of *BBC Hymn Book,* 1951

WOODLANDS   10 10 10 10

Unison

1   Hope of our calling: hope through courage won
    by those who dared to share all Christ had done.
    Saints of today, Christ's banner now unfurled,
    will bring his gospel to a waiting world.

2   Hope of our calling: hope with strength empowered,
    inspired by all that we have seen and heard;
    this call is ours, for we are chosen too,
    to live for God in all we say and do.

3   Hope of our calling: hope with grace outpoured,
    from death's despair the gift of life restored;
    our call to serve, to wash each other's feet,
    to bring Christ's healing touch to all we meet.

4   Hope of our calling: hope by faith made bold
    to sow God's righteousness throughout the world;
    bring peace from conflict, fruitfulness from weeds,
    the kingdom's harvest from the kingdom's seeds.

5   Hope of our calling: Spirit-filled, unbound,
    old joys remembered and new purpose found,
    our call refreshed by sacrament and word,
    we go in peace to love and serve the Lord.

ALLY BARRETT (*b.* 1975)

Music: WALTER GREATOREX (1877–1949)

HERE I AM, LORD

Music: DANIEL L. SCHUTTE (*b.* 1947)

1. I, the Lord of sea and sky,
    I have heard my people cry.
    All who dwell in dark and sin
        my hand will save.
    I, who made the stars of night,
    I will make their darkness bright.
    Who will bear my light to them?
    Whom shall I send?

    Here I am, Lord. Is it I, Lord?
    I have heard you calling in the night.
    I will go, Lord, if you lead me.
    I will hold your people in my heart.

2. I, the Lord of snow and rain,
    I have borne my people's pain.
    I have wept for love of them.
        They turn away.
    I will break their hearts of stone,
    give them hearts for love alone.
    I will speak my word to them.
    Whom shall I send?

3. I, the Lord of wind and flame,
    I will tend the poor and lame.
    I will set a feast for them.
        My hand will save.
    Finest bread I will provide
    till their hearts be satisfied.
    I will give my life to them.
    Whom shall I send?

DANIEL L. SCHUTTE (b. 1947)

GRAFTON (TANTUM ERGO SACRAMENTUM)   87 87 87

Music: French church melody from *Chants Ordinaires de l'Office Divin,*
Paris, 1881, *arranged by* SYDNEY HUGO NICHOLSON (1875–1947)

For ordination services

1   In the name of Christ we gather,
      in the name of Christ we sing,
    as we celebrate the promise
      of your servant's offering,
    here ordained to lead God's people
      at the gospel's beckoning.

2   Sons and daughters of the Spirit,
      we are called to teach and care,
    called as were the first disciples,
      commonwealth of Christ to share,
    and in bread and wine and water
      sacraments of grace declare.

3   In our preaching, praying, caring,
      may your word spring into life;
    in our time of doubt and challenge,
      may its truth affirm belief;
    and in days of pain and darkness,
      may it heal our guilt and grief.

4   Word of joy, enlivening Spirit,
      more than lover, parent, friend,
    born in Jesus, born in Mary,
      born in us, that love extend,
    grow within your chosen servant(s),
      life of God that has no end!

SHIRLEY ERENA MURRAY (*b.* 1931) *(alt.)*

The original hymn had five verses;
this version appears with the author's permission.

HYFRYDOL   87 87 D

Music: Melody by ROWLAND HUW PRICHARD (1811–1887)
harmonised by Compilers of *English Hymnal,* 1906

1 Long ago you taught your people:
  'Part of what you reap is mine —
from your cattle, bring the firstborn;
  tithe the crops of field and vine.'
Though beneath the Law's restrictions
  we are not compelled to live,
as we reap our monthly harvest,
  make us eager, Lord, to give.

2 What a way of life you showed us
  through the Son you gladly gave:
never snared by earthly treasure,
  buried in a borrowed grave —
yet to all he freely offered
  riches of the deepest kind:
let us live with his example
  firmly fixed in heart and mind.

3 In the life-style of the Spirit
  giving has a central part;
teach us, Lord, this grace of sharing
  with a cheerful, loving heart —
not a tiresome obligation,
  not a barren legal due,
but an overflow of worship:
  all we have belongs to you!

MARTIN LECKEBUSCH (b. 1962)

LONDONDERRY AIR   11 10 11 10 D

*Music: Irish traditional melody
        harmonised by* DONALD DAVISON (*b.* 1937)

1   Lord of the Church, we pray for our renewing:
       Christ over all, our undivided aim.
    Fire of the Spirit, burn for our enduing,
       wind of the Spirit, fan the living flame!
    We turn to Christ amid our fear and failing,
       the will that lacks the courage to be free,
    the weary labours, all but unavailing,
       to bring us nearer what a church should be.

2   Lord of the Church, we seek a Father's blessing,
       a true repentance and a faith restored,
    a swift obedience and a new possessing,
       filled with the Holy Spirit of the Lord!
    We turn to Christ from all our restless striving,
       unnumbered voices with a single prayer:
    the living water for our souls' reviving,
       in Christ to live, and love and serve and care.

3   Lord of the Church, we long for our uniting,
       true to one calling, by one vision stirred;
    one cross proclaiming and one creed reciting,
       one in the truth of Jesus and his word.
    So lead us on; till toil and trouble ended,
       one Church triumphant one new song shall sing,
    to praise his glory, risen and ascended,
       Christ over all, the everlasting King!

TIMOTHY DUDLEY-SMITH (b. 1926)

RUSTINGTON   87 87 D

1   Lord, you give the great commission:
      'Heal the sick and preach the word.'
    Lest the Church neglect its mission,
      and the gospel go unheard,
    help us witness to your purpose
      with renewed integrity;
        with the Spirit's gifts empower us
        for the work of ministry.

2   Lord, you call us to your service:
      'In my name baptize and teach.'
    That the world may trust your promise,
      life abundant meant for each,
    give us all new fervour, draw us
      closer in community;
        with the Spirit's gifts empower us
        for the work of ministry.

Music: CHARLES HUBERT HASTINGS PARRY (1848–1918)

3   Lord, you make the common holy:
      'This my body, this my blood.'
   Let us all, for earth's true glory,
      daily lift life heavenward,
   asking that the world around us
      share your children's liberty;
        with the Spirit's gifts empower us
        for the work of ministry.

4   Lord, you show us love's true measure;
      'Father, what they do, forgive.'
   Yet we hoard as private treasure
      all that you so freely give.
   May your care and mercy lead us
      to a just society;
        with the Spirit's gifts empower us
        for the work of ministry.

5   Lord, you bless with words assuring:
      'I am with you to the end.'
   Faith and hope and love restoring,
      may we serve as you intend,
   and, amid the cares that claim us,
      hold in mind eternity;
        with the Spirit's gifts empower us
        for the work of ministry.

JEFFERY W. ROWTHORN (b. 1934)

Refrain *

O Lord, you are the cen-tre of my life: I will al-ways praise you, I will al-ways serve you, I will al-ways keep you in my sight. O sight. sight.

First time ... *To verses* ... *Last time*

Cantor(s)

1 Keep me safe, O God, I take re-fuge in you. I say to the
2 I will bless the Lord who gives me coun-sel, who ev-en at
3 So my heart re-joi-ces, my soul is glad; ev-en in
4 You will show me the path of life, the full-ness of

Lord, 'You are my God. My hap-pi-ness
night di-rects my heart. I keep the Lord
safe-ty shall my bo-dy rest. For you will not leave my
joy in your pre-sence, at your right hand,

D.S.

lies in you a-lone; my hap-pi-ness lies in you a-lone.' O
ev-er in my sight: since he is at my right hand, I shall stand firm. O
soul a-mong the dead, nor let your be-lov-ed know de-cay. O

at your right hand hap-pi-ness for ev-er. O

PAUL INWOOD (b. 1947)
based on Psalm 16

* *The refrain is first sung by the Cantor, then repeated by All.*

Music: PAUL INWOOD (b. 1947)

PEACOCK

1 One is the bo - dy and one is the Head,
one is the Spi - rit by whom we are led; one God and
Fa - ther, one faith and one call for all._____
(4) to Christ our Lord.

1   One is the body and one is the Head,
one is the Spirit by whom we are led;
   one God and Father,
one faith and one call for all.

2   Christ who ascended to heaven above
is the same Jesus whose nature is love,
   who once descended
to bring to this earth new birth.

3   Gifts have been given well-suited to each,
some to be prophets, to pastor or preach,
   some, through the gospel,
to challenge, convert and teach.

4   Called to his service are women and men
so that his body might ever again
   witness through worship,
through deed and through word
   to Christ our Lord.

JOHN L. BELL *(b.1949)*
based on Ephesians 4.11-16

Music: JOHN L. BELL *(b.1949)*

1 Re - - store, O Lord, the ho - nour of your name! In works of sov - ereign po - wer come shake the earth a- - gain, that all may see, and come with rev - erent fear to the li - ving God,___ whose king - dom

vv. 1 - 3   *v. 4*

shall__ out - last the years. 2 Re - years.

2   Restore, O Lord, in all the earth your fame,
    and in our time revive
    the church that bears your name,
  and in your anger, Lord, remember mercy,
     O living God,
  whose mercy shall outlast the years.

3   Bend us, O Lord, where we are hard and cold,
    in your refiner's fire;
    come purify the gold:
  though suffering comes, and evil crouches near,
     still our living God
  is reigning, he is reigning here.

4   Restore, O Lord, the honour of your name!
    In works of sovereign power
    come shake the earth again,
  that all may see, and come with reverent fear
     to the living God,
  whose kingdom shall outlast the years.

GRAHAM KENDRICK (*b.* 1950)
and CHRIS ROLINSON (*b.* 1958)

Music: GRAHAM KENDRICK (*b.* 1950) and CHRIS ROLINSON (*b.* 1958)
arranged by DAVID PEACOCK (*b.* 1949)

LAUS DEO (REDHEAD NO 46)   87 87

1 Send, O God, your Holy Spirit
   on your people gathered here.
   Fill our lives with gentle courage;
   let your love cast out our fear.

2 Every perfect gift is given
   by the God whose name we bear
   to equip the saints of Jesus
   for the saving work we share.

3 Gifts of wisdom, gifts of knowledge,
   gifts of faith and healing grace,
   gifts that in the Spirit's power
   will reveal the Saviour's face.

4 All God's children, all Christ's people,
   all the saints, receive this word!
   Claim the gift, the faith, the promise,
   build the body of the Lord.

SYLVIA G. DUNSTAN (1955–1993)

Music: RICHARD REDHEAD (1820–1901)
Church Hymn Tunes, 1853
descant by PERCY WHITLOCK (1903–1946)

HOLY MANNA   87 87 and refrain

1   Summoned by the God who made us
      rich in our diversity,
    gathered in the name of Jesus,
      richer still in unity:

    Let us bring the gifts that differ
        and, in splendid, varied ways,
    sing a new Church into being,
        one in faith and love and praise.

2   Radiant risen from the water,
      robed in holiness and light,
    male and female in God's image,
      male and female, God's delight:

3   Trust the goodness of creation;
      trust the Spirit strong within,
    dare to dream the vision promised,
      sprung from seed of what has been.

4   Bring the hopes of every nation;
      bring the art of every race.
    Weave a song of peace and justice;
      let it sound through time and space.

5   Draw together at one table
      all the human family;
    shape a circle ever wider
      and a people ever free.

                              DELORES DUFNER, OSB

Music: The Columbian Harmony, Cincinatti, 1825
   arranged by DONALD DAVISON (b. 1937)

THORNBURY   76 76 D

1   Tell all the world of Jesus,
       our Saviour, Lord and King;
   and let the whole creation
       of his salvation sing:
   proclaim his glorious greatness
       in nature and in grace;
   Creator and Redeemer,
       the Lord of time and space.

2   Tell all the world of Jesus,
       that everyone may find
   the joy of his forgiveness —
       true peace of heart and mind:
   proclaim his perfect goodness,
       his deep, unfailing care;
   his love so rich in mercy,
       a love beyond compare.

3   Tell all the world of Jesus,
       that everyone may know
   of his almighty triumph
       defeating every foe:
   proclaim his coming glory,
       when sin is overthrown
   and he shall reign in splendour —
       the King upon his throne!

JAMES SEDDON (1915–1983)

Music: BASIL HARWOOD (1859–1949)

CHECKENDON

DCM and refrain

Turn over for v. 4 music and descant.

1   We need each other's voice to sing
　　　the songs our hearts would raise,
　　to set the whole world echoing
　　　with one great hymn of praise.
　　We blend our voices to complete
　　　the melody that starts
　　with God who sets and keeps the beat
　　　that stirs our loving hearts:

　　　　We give our alleluias
　　　　to the Church's common chord:
　　　　Alleluia! Alleluia!
　　　　Praise, O praise, O praise the Lord!

Music: JOHN BARNARD (*b.* 1948)

2   We need each other's strength to lift
the cross we're called to bear.
Each other's presence is a gift
of God's incarnate care.
When acts of love and tender speech
convey the Saviour's voice,
then praise exceeds what words can reach
and we with song rejoice:

3   We need each other's views to see
the limits of the mind,
that God in fact turns out to be
far more than we've defined,
that God's own image shines in all,
in every class and race,
and every group receives the call
to sing with faith and grace:

4   We need each other's voice to sing,
each other's strength to love,
each other's views to help us bring
our hearts to God above.
Our lives like coals placed side by side
to feed each other's flame,
shall with the Spirit's breath provide
a blaze of faith to claim:

THOMAS H. TROEGER (b. 1945)

4 We need each o-ther's voice to sing, each o-ther's strength to love,

each o-ther's views to help us bring our hearts to God a-bove.

Our lives like coals placed side by side to feed each o-ther's flame,

shall with the Spi-rit's breath pro-vide a blaze of faith to

Descant

claim: We give___ our___ al - le - lu - ias

claim: We give our al - le - lu - ias to the

to the Chur-ch's com-mon chord: Al - le - lu - ia!___

Chur-ch's com-mon chord: Al - le - lu - ia! Al - le -

___ Al - le - lu - - ia! Praise, O praise the Lord!

- lu - ia! Praise, O praise, O praise the Lord!

GLANHAFREN   64 64 6664

1   What shall our greeting be?
        Jesus is Lord!
    Sign of our unity?
        Jesus is Lord!
    May we no more defend
    barriers he died to end:
    give me your hand, my friend:
    one Church, one Lord!

2   What is our mission here?
        One world, one Lord!
    He makes his purpose clear:
        one world, one Lord!
    Spirit of truth descend,
    all our confusions end:
    give me your hand, my friend:
    Jesus is Lord!

3   He comes to save us now,
        Jesus our Lord!
    To serve him is to know
        life's true reward.
    May he our lives amend,
    all our betrayals end:
    give me your hand, my friend:
    Jesus is Lord!

FRED PRATT GREEN (1903–2000)

Music: Welsh hymn tune
    arranged by JOHN BARNARD (*b.* 1948)

KELVINGROVE   76 76 77 76

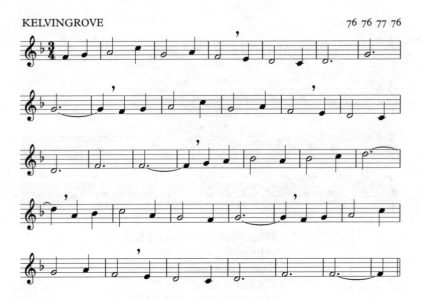

1   Will you come and follow me
       if I but call your name?
     Will you go where you don't know
       and never be the same?
     Will you let my love be shown,
       will you let my love be known,
   will you let my life be grown
       in you and you in me?

2   Will you leave yourself behind
       if I but call your name?
     Will you care for cruel and kind
       and never be the same?
     Will you risk the hostile stare
       should your life attract or scare?
     Will you let me answer prayer
       in you and you in me?

Music: Scottish folk melody
      arranged by JOHN L. BELL (*b.* 1949)

3   Will you let the blinded see
      if I but call your name?
      Will you set the prisoners free
      and never be the same?
      Will you kiss the leper clean,
      and do such as this unseen,
      and admit to what I mean
      in you and you in me?

4   Will you love the 'you' you hide
      if but call your name?
      Will you quell the fear inside
      and never be the same?
      Will you use the faith you've found
      to reshape the world around,
      through my sight and touch and sound
      in you and you in me?

5   Lord, your summons echoes true
      when you but call my name.
      Let me turn and follow you
      and never be the same.
      In your company I'll go
      where your love and footsteps show.
      Thus I'll move and live and grow
      in you and you in me.

JOHN L. BELL   (b. 1949)
and GRAHAM MAULE   (b. 1958)

171   Words: From *Heaven Shall Not Wait*, 1987. © 1987, Wild Goose Resource Group,
The Iona Community, 4th Floor, Savoy Centre, 140 Sauchiehall Street, Glasgow G2 3DH

HESLINGTON   11 10 11 10

1   Your voice, O God, outsings the stars of morning,
        your art in sky and season is displayed,
     your complex ways we trace in awe and wonder,
        and marvel — in your image we are made.

2   What can we say? Can words express our wonder?
        How shall we live? Can we reflect your grace?
     Come Spirit, come, disturb our cautious living,
        be known in us, your human dwelling place.

3   You call your Church from every land and nation;
        you reconcile, for we in Christ are one.
     We yearn to see creation's full redemption:
        all things restored in Christ, the risen Son.

4   O holy God, we worship and adore you,
        your Word made flesh shared human joy and strife,
     in him you draw us in love's dance of freedom:
        your Church, your people, in your common life.

ROSALIND BROWN   (b. 1953)

Music: RICHARD SHEPHARD (b. 1949)

173

GATHERING

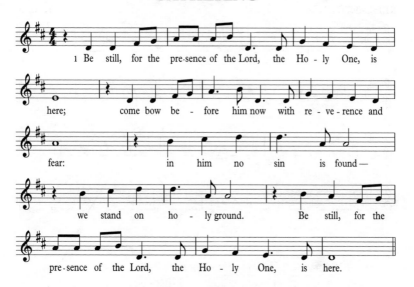

1 Be still, for the presence of the Lord, the Holy One, is here; come bow before him now with reverence and fear: in him no sin is found — we stand on holy ground. Be still, for the presence of the Lord, the Holy One, is here.

2   Be still, for the glory of the Lord
        is shining all around;
    he burns with holy fire,
        with splendour he is crowned:
    how awesome is the sight —
    our radiant King of light!
    Be still, for the glory of the Lord
        is shining all around.

3   Be still, for the power of the Lord
        is moving in this place:
    he comes to cleanse and heal,
        to minister his grace.
    No work too hard for him,
    in faith receive from him.
    Be still, for the power of the Lord
        is moving in this place.

DAVID J. EVANS (b. 1957)

Music: DAVID J. EVANS (b. 1957)

REDLAND   74 74 D

GATHERING

1   Bring to God your new, best songs,
      all creation;
  raise a hymn of gratitude
      for salvation;
  far and wide, throughout the world,
      sound his glory;
  he has done amazing things —
      tell the story.

2   Earth and heavens, revere the Lord,
      your Creator;
  why exalt some other God?
      He is greater!
  His are strength and majesty
      never ending;
  ours, the privilege of praise,
      voices blending.

3   With the finest you possess
      bow before him;
  from the fullness of your heart,
      come, adore him.
  See, his beauty floods the earth —
      holy splendour!
  Yield to him in holy fear —
      glad surrender!

4   All that lurks in human hearts
      he discloses;
  all that fails the test of truth
      he opposes.
  Let the earth rejoice in hope
      of his kingdom;
  skies and oceans, trees and fields,
      join the anthem!

MARTIN LECKEBUSCH (b. 1962)
based on Psalm 96

174   Words: © 2000, Kevin Mayhew Ltd, Buxhall, Stowmarket, Suffolk IP14 3BW   Used by permission.

GATHER US IN

1 Here in this place new light is stream-ing, now is the dark-ness van-ished a-way; see in this space our fears and our dream-ings brought here to you in the light of this day. _____

Gath-er us in, the lost and for-sak-en, gath-er us in, the blind and the lame: call to us now and we shall a-wak-en, we shall a-rise at the sound of our name. _____

Music: MARTY HAUGEN (b. 1950)

1   Here in this place new light is streaming,
    now is the darkness vanished away:
  see in this space our fears and our dreamings
    brought here to you in the light of this day.
  Gather us in, the lost and forsaken,
    gather us in, the blind and the lame:
  call to us now and we shall awaken,
    we shall arise at the sound of our name.

2   We are the young, our lives are a mystery;
    we are the old who yearn for your face;
  we have been sung throughout all of history,
    called to be light to the whole human race.
  Gather us in, the rich and the haughty,
    gather us in, the proud and the strong:
  give us a heart so meek and so lowly,
    give us the courage to enter the song.

3   Here we will take the wine and the water,
    here we will take the bread of new birth:
  here you shall call your sons and your daughters,
    call us anew to be salt for the earth.
  Give us to drink the wine of compassion,
    give us to eat the bread that is you:
  nourish us well and teach us to fashion
    lives that are holy and hearts that are true.

4   Not in the dark of buildings confining,
    not in some heaven light-years away,
  but here in this place the new light is shining,
    now is the kingdom, and now is the day.
  Gather us in and hold us for ever,
    gather us in and make us your own,
  gather us in, all peoples together —
    fire of your love in our flesh and our bone.

MARTY HAUGEN (b. 1950)

TWO OAKS

1 Let us build a house where love can dwell and all can safely live,—

a place where saints and chil-dren— tell how—

hearts learn— to for-give. Built of hopes and dreams and

vi-sions, rock of faith and vault of grace; here the

love of Christ shall end di-vi-sions: *all are wel-come,*

all are wel-come, all are wel-come in this

vv. 1-4 | *v. 5*

place.—

1   Let us build a house where love can dwell
     and all can safely live,
   a place where saints and children tell
     how hearts learn to forgive.
   Built of hopes and dreams and visions,
     rock of faith and vault of grace;
   here the love of Christ shall end divisions:

     all are welcome, all are welcome,
     all are welcome in this place.

Music: MARTY HAUGEN (b. 1950)

2   Let us build a house where prophets speak,
       and words are strong and true,
    where all God's children dare to seek
       to dream God's reign anew.
    Here the cross shall stand as witness
       and as symbol of God's grace;
    here as one we claim the faith of Jesus:

3   Let us build a house where love is found
       in water, wine and wheat:
    a banquet hall on holy ground,
       where peace and justice meet.
    Here the love of God, through Jesus,
       is revealed in time and space;
    as we share in Christ the feast that frees us:

4   Let us build a house where hands will reach
       beyond the wood and stone
    to heal and strengthen, serve and teach,
       and live the Word they've known.
    Here the outcast and the stranger
       bear the image of God's face;
    let us bring an end to fear and danger:

5   Let us build a house where all are named,
       their songs and visions heard
    and loved and treasured, taught and claimed
       as words within the Word.
    Built of tears and cries and laughter,
       prayers of faith and songs of grace,
    let this house proclaim from floor to rafter:

MARTY HAUGEN (b. 1950)

176 Words and Music: © 1994, GIA Publications Inc., 7404 S. Mason Avenue, Chicago, IL 60638, USA. www.giamusic.com

TOR HILL   87 87 D

1   Living God, your word has called us,
          summoned us to live by grace,
      make us one in hope and vision,
          as we gather in this place.
      Take our searching, take our praising,
          take the silence of our prayer,
      offered up in joyful worship,
          springing from the love we share.

2   Living God, your love has called us
          in the name of Christ your Son,
      forming us to be his body,
          by your Spirit making one.
      Working, laughing, learning, growing,
          old and young and black and white,
      gifts and skills together sharing,
          in your service all unite.

3   Living God, your hope has called us
          to the world that you have made,
      teaching us to live for others,
          humble, joyful, unafraid.
      Give us eyes to see your presence,
          joy in laughter, hope in pain.
      In our loving, in our living,
          give us strength that Christ may reign.

JAN BERRY (b. 1953)

Music: MALCOLM ARCHER (b. 1952)

177   Words: © 1999, Kevin Mayhew Ltd, Buxhall, Stowmarket, Suffolk IP14 3BW   Used by permission.
177   Music: © Malcolm Archer

CHARIS   12 12 13 and refrain

De - - o gra - ti - as,   De - - o gra - ti - as,

thanks   be   to   God   most   high.

1 Thanks be to God whose love has gathered us today;
   thanks be to God who helps and guides us on our way.
   Thanks be to God who gives us voice that we may thank him:

   Deo gratias, Deo gratias, thanks be to God most high.

2 Thanks be to God for all the gifts of life and light;
   thanks be to God whose care protects us day and night.
   Thanks be to God who keeps in mind us who forget him:

3 Thanks be to God who knows our secret joys and fears;
   thanks be to God who, when we call him, always hears.
   Thanks be to God our rock and strength ever sustaining:

4 Thanks be to God who never turns his face away;
   thanks be to God who heals and pardons all who stray.
   Thanks be to God who welcomes us into the Kingdom:

5 Thanks be to God who made our world and all we see;
   thanks be to God who gave his Son to set us free.
   Thanks be to God whose Spirit brings warmth and rejoicing:

                                    STEPHEN DEAN (*b.* 1948)

           'Deo gratias' — 'Thanks be to God.'

Music: STEPHEN DEAN (*b.* 1948)

Music: ALEXANDER GONDO
transcribed by I-TO LOH
arranged by JOHN L. BELL (*b.* 1949)

ALEXANDER GONDO
Original Shona text *Uyai mose*
English paraphrase by I-TO LOH

PENITENCE

65 65

1 Bright as fire in darkness,
   sharper than a sword,
   lives throughout the ages
   God's eternal Word.

2 Christ, your eyes of mercy
   see our sins revealed;
   speak the word that saves us,
   that we may be healed.

3 Father, Son and Spirit,
   Trinity of might,
   compassed in your glory,
   give the world your light.

Stanbrook Abbey

Music: JOHN BARNARD (*b.* 1948)

Father, hear our prayer
that our lives may be
consecrated only unto you;
cleanse us with your fire,
fill us with your power
that the world may glorify your name.
  Lord, have mercy on us.
  Christ, have mercy on us.
  Lord, have mercy on us.

ANDY PIERCY (b. 1951)

Music: ANDY PIERCY (b. 1951)

1 Purify my heart, let me be as gold and precious silver. Purify my heart, let me be as gold, pure gold.

Refrain

Refiner's fire, my heart's one desire is to be holy, set apart for you, Lord. I choose to be holy, set apart for you, my Master, ready to do your will.

2   Purify my heart,
    cleanse me from within and make me holy.
    Purify my heart,
    cleanse me from my sin, deep within.

    Refiner's fire, my heart's one desire
    is to be holy, set apart for you, Lord.
    I choose to be holy, set apart for you, my Master,
    ready to do your will.

BRIAN DOERKSEN *(b. 1965)*

Music: BRIAN DOERKSEN *(b. 1965)*

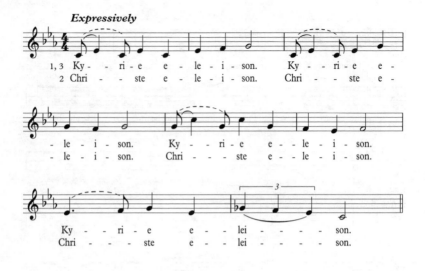

1   Kyrie eleison. Kyrie eleison.
     Kyrie eleison. Kyrie eleison.

2   Christe eleison. Christe eleison.
     Christe eleison. Christe eleison.

3   Kyrie eleison. Kyrie eleison.
     Kyrie eleison. Kyrie eleison.

Lord, have mercy. Christ, have mercy.

Liturgical text

The original setting consists of the Kyrie verse only.

Music: DINAH REINDORF (*b. c.* 1927)
          arranged by GEOFF WEAVER (*b.* 1943)

1 Kyrie eleison.
   Kyrie eleison.
   Kyrie eleison.

2 Christe eleison
   Christe eleison
   Christe eleison.

3 Kyrie eleison.
   Kyrie eleison.
   Kyrie eleison.

Lord, have mercy.
Christ, have mercy.

Liturgical text

The original setting consists of the Kyrie verse only.

Music: Ukrainian traditional chant

THE WORD OF GOD

GOWANBANK   87 87 D

1   God has spoken — by his prophets,
        spoken his unchanging word;
    each from age to age proclaiming
        God the one, the righteous Lord;
    in the world's despair and turmoil
        one firm anchor still holds fast:
    God is King, his throne eternal,
        God the first and God the last.

2   God has spoken — by Christ Jesus,
        Christ, the everlasting Son;
    brightness of the Father's glory,
        with the Father ever one:
    spoken by the Word incarnate,
        Life, before all time began,
    Light of Light, to earth descending,
        God, revealed as Son of Man.

3   God is speaking — by his Spirit
        speaking to our hearts again;
    in the age-long word expounding
        God's own message, now as then.
    Through the rise and fall of nations
        one sure faith is standing fast:
    God abides, his word unchanging,
        God the first and God the last.

GEORGE WALLACE BRIGGS (1875–1959)

Music: JOHN BARNARD (b. 1948)

FRAGRANCE   98 98 98

1   God in his wisdom, for our learning,
         gave his inspired and holy word:
     promise of Christ, for our discerning,
         by which our souls are moved and stirred,
     finding our hearts within us burning
         when, as of old, his voice is heard.

2   Symbol and story, song and saying,
         life-bearing truths for heart and mind,
     God in his sovereign grace displaying
         tenderest care for humankind,
     Jesus our Lord this love portraying,
         open our eyes to seek and find.

3   Come then with prayer and contemplation,
         see how in Scripture Christ is known;
     wonder anew at such salvation
         here in these sacred pages shown;
     lift every heart in adoration,
         children of God by grace alone!

                              TIMOTHY DUDLEY-SMITH (b. 1926)

Music: French traditional melody
    harmonised by PETER MOGER (b. 1964)

1 Speak, O Lord, as we come to you to receive the food of your holy word. Take your truth, plant it deep in us; shape and fashion us in your likeness, that the light of Christ might be seen today in our acts of love and our deeds of faith. Speak, O Lord, and fulfil in us all your purposes, for your glory.

2 Teach us, Lord, full obedience,
holy reverence, true humility.
Test our thoughts and our attitudes
in the radiance of your purity.
Cause our faith to rise, cause our eyes to see
your majestic love and authority.
Words of power that can never fail;
let their truth prevail over unbelief.

3 Speak, O Lord, and renew our minds;
help us grasp the heights of your plans for us.
Truths unchanged from the dawn of time
that will echo down through eternity.
And by grace we'll stand on your promises,
and by faith we'll walk as you walk with us.
Speak, O Lord, till your Church is built
and the earth is filled with your glory.

KEITH GETTY (b. 1974)
and STUART TOWNEND (b. 1963)

Music: KEITH GETTY (b. 1974) and STUART TOWNEND (b. 1963)

SKYE BOAT SONG   86 86 and refrain

Spirit of God, unseen as the wind,
gentle as is the dove,
teach us the truth and help us believe,
show us the Saviour's love.

1   You spoke to us long, long ago,
        gave us the written word;
     we read it still, needing its truth,
        through it God's voice is heard.

2   Without your help we fail our Lord,
        we cannot live his way;
     we need your power, we need your strength,
        following Christ each day.

MARGARET V. OLD (1932–2001)

Music: Scottish folk melody
    arranged by PETER NARDONE (*b.* 1965)

188   Words: © Scripture Union, 207-209 Queensway, Bletchley, Milton Keynes, Buckinghamshire.   MK2 2EB
          From *Sing to God*

GOSPEL GREETING

Refrain *

Al - le - - lu - ia! Your words, O Lord, are
spi - rit and life. Al - le - - lu - ia!

First time   D.S. | *To verse* | *Last time*

O - pen our hearts to your word._____   word._____   word._____

Cantor(s)

(*Advent*) Pre - pare a way for the Lord._____ Make God's
(*Christmas*) To - day a Sa - viour is born_____ who is
(*Easter*) Re - joice and sing, all the earth,_____ for the

path - - way straight,_____ and all the earth shall
Christ the Lord._____ God's Word is with us and
night is gone!_____ Our God has raised_ us

D.S.

see the sav - - ing love_____ of_ God._____
lives a - mong us with - in_____ our_ world._____
up from death in Christ Je - - sus the Son._____

BERNADETTE FARRELL (*b.* 1957)

* The refrain is first sung by the Cantor, then repeated by All.

Music: BERNADETTE FARRELL (*b.* 1957)

PILGRIM'S ALLELUIA

Refrain *

Al - le - lu - - ia,   al - le - lu - - ia,

al - le - lu - ia, _____ al - le - lu - ia.   *Fine*

Cantor(s)   Optional descant

1 Strong is your love.   Migh - ty your word.

1 Strong is your love.   Migh - ty your word.   Speak to us

Speak to us now,   Al - le - lu - - ia.   *D.S.*

now,   o - pen our hearts,   Al - le - lu - - ia.

2   Spirit of God, come fill our hearts.
     Message of truth, here among us,
     Alleluia.

3   All-holy God: Father of light,
     Word in our midst, Spirit and life:
     Alleluia.

4   Mighty is God, holy his name.
     Be here with us, teach us your way,
     Alleluia.

JAMES WALSH   (*b.* 1940)

* The refrain is first sung by the Cantor, then repeated by All.*
One or more verses may be sung.

Music: JAMES WALSH (*b.* 1940)

190 Words and Music: © 1997 James Walsh OSB. Published by OCP Publications, 5536 NE Hassalo, Portland, OR 97213,

WORD OF TRUTH AND LIFE

Cantor:

1 Praise the God of all creation,
   God of mercy and compassion:
   Alleluia! Alleluia!
   Praise the Word of Truth and Life!

2 Tree of life and endless wisdom,
   be our root, our growth and glory:
   Alleluia! Alleluia!
   Praise the Word of Truth and Life!

3 Living water, we are thirsting
   for the life that you have promised:
   Alleluia! Alleluia!
   Praise the Word of Truth and Life!

4 Gentle shepherd, you who know us,
   call us all into your presence:
   Alleluia! Alleluia!
   Praise the Word of Truth and Life!

MARTY HAUGEN (b. 1950)

One or more verses may be sung as a Gospel acclamation;
if sung as a complete song, verse 1 may be repeated at the end.

Music: MARTY HAUGEN (b. 1950)

CANTICLES and AFFIRMATIONS of FAITH

LUX EOI   87 87 D

1   We believe in God the Father,
      God almighty, by whose plan
    earth and heaven sprang to being,
      all created things began.
    We believe in Christ the Saviour,
      Son of God in human frame,
    virgin-born, the child of Mary
      upon whom the Spirit came.

2   Christ, who on the cross forsaken,
      like a lamb to slaughter led,
    suffered under Pontius Pilate,
      he descended to the dead.
    We believe in Jesus risen,
      heaven's king to rule and reign,
    to the Father's side ascended
      till as judge he comes again.

3   We believe in God the Spirit;
      in one Church, below, above:
    saints of God in one communion,
      one in holiness and love.
    So by faith, our sins forgiven,
      Christ our Saviour, Lord and friend,
    we shall rise with him in glory
      to the life that knows no end.

TIMOTHY DUDLEY-SMITH (b. 1926)
based on *The Apostles' Creed*

Music: ARTHUR SEYMOUR SULLIVAN (1842–1900)

DARWALL'S 148th

6 6 12 4 12

Music: JOHN DARWALL (1731–1789)
    descant by WILLIAM HENRY MONK (1823–1889)

1 All nations of the world
   be joyful in the Lord:
  with willing hands your Master serve with one accord:
   in ceaseless praise
  with heart and voice in him rejoice through all your days.

2 Be sure the Lord is God,
   creation's Source and Spring:
  in him alone we live, to him our lives we bring.
   From days of old
  he feeds his flock and guides the wanderers to his fold.

3 In gladness go your way:
   approach his courts with song
  in thankfulness to him to whom all things belong.
   His name adore:
  his gracious mercy, truth and love for evermore.

EDWIN LE GRICE (1911–1992)
based on Psalm 100 *(Jubilate Deo, A Song of Joy)*

Some or all of the optional verses, for one or more cantors, may be added once the ostinato has been sung at least twice.

Music: JACQUES BERTHIER (1923–1994)

crowns you with love and com - pas - sion. 5 The Lord is com-pas-sion and love, the Lord is pa-tient and rich in mer - cy. God does not treat us ac-cord-ing to our sins nor re - pay us ac-cord-ing to our faults. 6 As a Fa-ther has com-pas-sion on his child - ren, the Lord has mer - cy on those who re - vere him; for God knows of what we are made, and re - mem-bers that we are dust. 7 As__ the__ hea-vens are high a - bove the__ earth, so is God's way a-bove our__ way, so is God's__ love for us. 8 All your works are__ ho - ly, for you are our God; you bring jus - - tice to the op - pressed. 9 From ev-er-last - ing to ev - er-last - ing your__ love is for those who__ re - vere you.

Taizé Community
based on Psalm 103

194 Words and Music: © 1998, Ateliers et Presses de Taizé, 71250 Taizé, France

HOPE PARK   87 87 D

Music: IAN SHARP (*b.* 1943)

195   Music: © 2001, Stainer & Bell Ltd, 23 Gruneisen Road, London N3 1DZ   <www.stainer.co.uk>

1 Bless the Lord, the God of Israel,
    who has come to set us free.
   He has raised for us a Saviour
    sprung from royal David's tree.
   Through his prophets God had spoken
    of the hope the Christ would bring;
   of his faithfulness and mercy
    let each generation sing.

2 Long ago God made a promise
    he would set his people free,
   that in all our life and worship
    we might know true liberty,
   to be holy, to be righteous
    in his sight throughout our days;
   now this child will be a herald
    making ready all God's ways.

3 Let all people know salvation
    through forgiveness of their sin,
   as our God in his compassion
    bids a shining dawn begin.
   So may all who dwell in darkness
    see the shadows disappear
   while he guides our feet in pathways
    where his peace is ever near.

4 *(Second half of tune)*
   To the Father be all glory
    with the Spirit and the Son,
   as it was, is now and shall be
    while eternal ages run.

ANNE HARRISON (*b.*1954)
based on Luke 1.68-79
(Benedictus, The Song of Zechariah)

Music: OWEN ALSTOTT (*b.* 1947)

My soul rejoices in God, my Saviour.
My spirit finds its joy in God, the living God.

1 My soul proclaims your mighty deeds.
My spirit sings the greatness of your name.

2 Your mercy flows throughout the land
and every generation knows your love.

3 You cast the mighty from their thrones
and raise the poor and lowly to new life.

4 You fill the hungry with good things.
With empty hands you send the rich away.

5 Just as you promised Abraham,
you come to free your people, Israel.

based on Luke 1.46-55 *(Magnificat, The Song of Mary)*

OWEN ALSTOTT *(b.* 1947)

NORTH BAILEY

CM

Music: PETER MOGER (*b.* 1964)

1   With Mary let my soul rejoice,
     and praise God's holy name —
     his saving love from first to last,
     from age to age, the same!

2   How strong his arm, how great his power!
     The proud he will disown;
     the meek and humble he exalts
     to share his glorious throne.

3   The rich our God will send away
     and feed the hungry poor;
     the arms of love remain outstretched
     at mercy's open door.

4   So shall God's promise be fulfilled,
     to Israel firmly made:
     a child is born, a Son is given
     whose crown will never fade.

5   All glory to the Father, Son
     and Spirit now proclaim;
     with Mary let the world rejoice
     and praise God's holy name!

DAVID MOWBRAY (b. 1938)
based on Luke 1.46-55 *(Magnificat, The Song of Mary)*

NORTH COATES   65 65

1   Lord, now let your servant
        go his way in peace —
     your great love has brought me
        joy that will not cease.

2   For my eyes have seen him
        promised from of old —
     saviour of all people,
        shepherd of one fold.

3   Light of revelation
        to the Gentiles shown,
     light of Israel's glory
        to the world made known.

JAMES SEDDON (1915–1983)
based on Luke 2.29-32
(Nunc Dimittis, The Song of Simeon)

Music: TIMOTHY RICHARD MATTHEWS (1826–1910)

ST PAUL'S   SM

1   Lord, set your servant free,
        fulfil your ancient vow,
   and peaceful let the parting be
      which seals that promise now.

2   For here the child of light,
        the world's salvation lies,
   and on the nations lost in night
      I see his dawn arise.

3   A radiance unconfined
       to change of time or place,
   he is the hope of humankind,
     the glory of our race.

MARY HOLTBY
based on Luke 2.29-32
(Nunc Dimittis, The Song of Simeon)

Music: JOHN STAINER (1840–1901)

CELTIC ALLELUIA

Music: FINTAN O'CARROLL (1922–1981) and CHRISTOPHER WALKER (b. 1947)

Alleluia, alleluia.
Alleluia, alleluia.

1   Father we praise you as Lord,
    all of the earth gives you worship,
    for your majesty fills the heavens, fills the earth.

2   Blessed apostles sing praise;
    prophets and martyrs give glory:
    'For your majesty praise the Spirit, praise the Son!'

3   You are the Christ everlasting,
    born for us all of a Virgin,
    you have conquered death, opened heaven to all believers.

4   Help those you saved by your blood,
    raise them to life with your martyrs.
    Save your people, Lord, as their ruler raise them up.

FINTAN O'CARROLL (1922–1981)
and CHRISTOPHER WALKER (b. 1947)
based on *Te Deum laudamus (A Song of the Church)*

RUSTINGTON   87 87 D

Music: CHARLES HUBERT HASTINGS PARRY (1848–1918)

1   God, we praise you, God, we bless you!
    God, we name you sovereign Lord!
    Mighty King whom angels worship,
        Father, by your Church adored:
    all creation shows your glory,
        heaven and earth draw near your throne,
    singing, 'Holy, holy, holy,
        Lord of hosts, and God alone!'

2   True apostles, faithful prophets,
        saints who set their world ablaze,
    martyrs, once unknown, unheeded,
        join one growing song of praise,
    while your Church on earth confesses
        one majestic Trinity:
    Father, Son and Holy Spirit,
        God, our hope eternally.

3   Jesus Christ, the King of glory,
        everlasting Son of God,
    humble was your virgin mother,
        hard the lonely path you trod.
    By your cross is sin defeated,
        hell confronted face to face,
    heaven opened to believers,
        sinners justified by grace.

4   Christ, at God's right hand victorious,
        you will judge the world you made;
    Lord, in mercy help your servants
        for whose freedom you have paid.
    Raise us up from dust to glory,
        guard us from all sin today;
    King enthroned above all praises,
        save your people, God, we pray!

CHRISTOPHER IDLE (b. 1938)
based on *Te Deum laudamus* (*A Song of the Church*)

SICILIAN MARINERS 87 87

1 Glory, honour, endless praises
 here we offer, King of kings.
 You are source of all our being,
 Lord of all created things.

2 Glory, honour, endless praises
 to the Lamb who has been slain:
 by your blood you ransomed sinners,
 set your people free again.

3 Called to serve from every nation,
 kings and priests, we praise you, Lord,
 and to Father and to Spirit
 lift our hearts with one accord.

EDWIN LE GRICE (1911–1992)
based on Revelation 4, 5 *(A Song of Praise)*

Music: 18th-century Italian melody in Tattersall's *Improved Psalmody* 1792
harmonised by DONALD DAVISON (b. 1937)

WÜRTTEMBERG (NASSAU)   77 77 6

1   Great and wonderful your deeds,
        God, from whom all power proceeds:
    true and right are all your ways —
        who shall not give thanks and praise?
        To your name be glory!

2   King of nations, take your crown!
        Every race shall soon bow down:
    holy Lord and God alone,
        justice in your deeds is shown;
        all have seen your glory.

3   To the one almighty God,
        to the Lamb who shed his blood,
    to the Spirit now be given,
        by the hosts of earth and heaven,
        love and praise and glory!

CHRISTOPHER IDLE (b. 1938)
based on Revelation 15.3-4 (Great and Wonderful)

Music: Melody from *Hundert Arien,* Dresden 1694
    adapted by WILLIAM HENRY MONK (1823–1889)

PRAYER

Steadily

Refrain

There is a long-ing in our hearts, O Lord, for you to re-veal your-self to us.____ There is a long-ing in our hearts for

(pause last time)

love we on-ly find in you, our God.

1 For jus-tice, for free-dom, for mer-cy: hear our prayer.____ In sor-row, in grief: be near, hear our prayer, O God.

Fine

D.S.

Music: ANNE QUIGLEY

PRAYER

There is a longing in our hearts, O Lord,
for you to reveal yourself to us.
There is a longing in our hearts for love
we only find in you, our God.

1   For justice, for freedom,
    for mercy: hear our prayer.
      In sorrow, in grief:
    be near, hear our prayer, O God.

2   For wisdom, for courage,
    for comfort: hear our prayer.
      In weakness, in fear:
    be near, hear our prayer, O God.

3   For healing, for wholeness,
    for new life: hear our prayer.
      In sickness, in death:
    be near, hear our prayer, O God.

4   Lord save us, take pity,
    light in our darkness.
      We call you, we wait:
    be near, hear our prayer, O God.

ANNE QUIGLEY

204 Words and Music: © 1992 Anne Quigley. Published by OCP Publications, 5536 NE Hassalo, Portland, OR 97213, USA.
All rights reserved. Used with permission.

Cantor ... *All*

Lord, hear our cry: Lis-ten to our prayer.

Cantor:
Lord, hear our cry:
All:
Listen to our prayer.

Music: JOHN L. BELL (*b.* 1949)   JOHN L. BELL (*b.* 1949)

206

Through our lives and— by our prayers, your king-dom come.

Through our lives and by our prayers,
your kingdom come.

JOHN L. BELL (*b.* 1949)
Music: JOHN L. BELL (*b.* 1949)   and GRAHAM MAULE (*b.* 1958)

207

Lord, in your mer - - cy hear our prayer.

Lord, in your mercy hear our prayer.

Liturgical text

A cantor may sing 'Lord, in your mercy'
to which all respond, 'hear our prayer.'

Music: JOHN HARPER (*b.* 1947)

My eyes are dim with weep-ing and my pil-low soaked with

tears. Faith-ful God, re-mem-ber me.

Cantor:
My eyes are dim with weeping
and my pillow soaked with tears.
All:
Faithful God, remember me.

Music: ALISON ADAM (*b.* 1960)
        arranged by JOHN L. BELL (*b.* 1949)   ALISON ADAM (*b.* 1960)

We ask you, Lord, lis-ten to our prayer.

We ask you, Lord, lis-ten to our prayer.

Cantor:
We ask you, Lord,
All:
listen to our prayer.
Cantor:
We ask you, Lord,
All:
listen to our prayer.

Music: PAUL INWOOD (*b.* 1947)   PAUL INWOOD (*b.* 1947)

MAYENZIWE

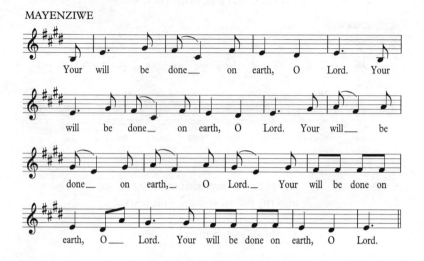

Your will be done on earth, O Lord.
Your will be done on earth, O Lord.
Your will be done on earth, O Lord.
Your will be done on earth, O Lord.
Your will be done on earth, O Lord.

Original Xhosa text:
Mazenziwe 'ntando yakho.

Xhosa (South African) text,
from *The Lord's Prayer*

Music: South African traditional, as taught by George Mxadana and transcribed in 1988 by John Bell.

HOLY COMMUNION

LAYING DOWN

10 10 10 4

1   Before I take the body of my Lord,
    before I share his life in bread and wine,
    I recognize the sorry things within:
        these I lay down.

2   The words of hope I often failed to give,
    the prayers of kindness buried by my pride,
    the signs of care I argued out of sight:
        these I lay down.

3   The narrowness of vision and of mind,
    the need for other folk to serve my will,
    and every word and silence meant to hurt:
        these I lay down.

4   Of those around in whom I meet my Lord,
    I ask their pardon and I grant them mine,
    that every contradiction of Christ's peace
        might be laid down.

5   Lord Jesus Christ, companion at this feast,
    I empty now my heart and stretch my hands,
    and ask to meet you here in bread and wine
        which you lay down.

JOHN L. BELL (b. 1949)
and GRAHAM MAULE (b. 1958)

Music: JOHN L. BELL (b. 1949)

211   Words and Music: From *Love From Below*, 1989. © 1989, Wild Goose Resource Group,
The Iona Community, 4th Floor, Savoy Centre, 140 Sauchiehall Street, Glasgow G2 3DH

1 Be-hold the Lamb who bears our sins a-way, slain for us:
and we re-mem-ber the pro-mise made that all who come in
faith find for-give-ness at the cross. So we share in this
bread of life, and we drink of his sa-cri-fice, as a
sign of our bonds of peace a-round the ta-ble of the

vv. 1 - 3   *v. 4*

King.   King.

Music: KEITH GETTY (*b.*1974), KRISTYN GETTY (*b.*1980)
and STUART TOWNEND (*b.*1963)

1. Behold the Lamb who bears our sins away,
   slain for us: and we remember
   the promise made that all who come in faith
   find forgiveness at the cross.
   So we share in this bread of life,
   and we drink of his sacrifice,
   as a sign of our bonds of peace
   around the table of the King.

2. The body of our Saviour, Jesus Christ,
   torn for you: eat and remember
   the wounds that heal, the death that brings us life,
   paid the price to make us one.
   So we share in this bread of life,
   and we drink of his sacrifice,
   as a sign of our bonds of love
   around the table of the King.

3. The blood that cleanses every stain of sin,
   shed for you: drink and remember
   he drained death's cup that all may enter in
   to receive the life of God.
   So we share in this bread of life,
   and we drink of his sacrifice,
   as a sign of our bonds of grace
   around the table of the King.

4. And so with thankfulness and faith we rise
   to respond and to remember
   our call to follow in the steps of Christ
   as his Body here on earth.
   As we share in his suffering,
   we proclaim: Christ will come again!
   And we'll join in the feast of heaven
   around the table of the King.

KEITH GETTY (b. 1974),
KRISTYN GETTY (b. 1980)
and STUART TOWNEND (b. 1963)

ABERYSTWYTH   77 77 D

1   Body broken for our good,
       and that body's precious blood:
    we receive them to our shame,
    who dishonour Jesus' name.
    Every day more blood is shed;
    flesh is broken, left for dead.
    Where earth's children bleed and die,
       it is Christ we crucify.

2   Yet your love, God, draws us near,
       though unworthy to be here;
    we have nothing good to bring,
       yet you give us everything!
    Here you give us Christ who died,
       resurrected, glorified;
    his humanity, divine,
       here is ours in bread and wine.

* 3 In communion with this Lord,
       faith, hope, love are all restored;
    here is wealth beyond compare,
       wealth for all the world to share.
    He reclaims our every breath:
       all our life and even death
    cannot be too great a price,
       to complete his sacrifice.

Music: JOSEPH PARRY (1841–1903)

4   Time, with energy and health,
        talent, poverty or wealth:
    all are yours, Lord, taken up
        in the sign of bread and cup.
    Though we may be broken too,
        and our lives poured out for you,
    make of us the living sign
        of your love in bread and wine.

ALAN GAUNT (b.1935)

214

GRACE IN ESSENCE   65 63

1   Bread is blessed and broken,
        wine is blessed and poured:
    take this and remember
            Christ the Lord.

2   Share the food of heaven
        earth cannot afford.
    Here is grace in essence —
            Christ the Lord.

3   Know yourself forgiven,
        find yourself restored,
    meet a friend for ever —
            Christ the Lord.

4   God has kept his promise
        sealed by sign and word:
    here, for those who want him —
            Christ the Lord.

JOHN L. BELL (b.1949)
and GRAHAM MAULE (b.1958)

Music: JOHN L. BELL (b.1949)

214 Words and Music: From *Love From Below*, 1989. © 1989, Wild Goose Resource Group,
The Iona Community, 4th Floor, Savoy Centre, 140 Sauchiehall Street, Glasgow G2 3DH

Bread of life, hope of the world,
Jesus Christ, our brother:
feed us now, give us life,
lead us to one another.

1   As we proclaim your death,
as we recall your life,
we remember your promise
to return again.

2   This bread we break and share
was scattered once as grain:
just as now it is gathered,
make your people one.

3   We eat this living bread,
we drink this saving cup:
sign of hope in our broken world,
source of lasting love.

Music: BERNADETTE FARRELL (b. 1957)

Additional or alternative verses:

4   Hold us in unity,
    in love for all to see;
    that the world may believe in you,
    God of all who live.

5   You are the bread of peace,
    you are the wine of joy,
    broken now for your people,
    poured in endless love.

Advent:

6   Be with your people, Lord,
    send us your saving Word:
    Jesus Christ, light of gladness,
    come among us now.

Christmas:

7   A Child is born for us,
    a Son is given to us,
    in our midst, Christ, our Lord and God
    come as one who serves.

Lent:

8   Our hunger for your word,
    our thirsting for your truth
    are the sign of your life in us
    till we rest in you.

BERNADETTE FARRELL (*b.* 1957)

215 Words and Music: © 1982 Bernadette Farrell. Published by OCP Publications,
5536 NE Hassalo, Portland, OR 97213, USA. All rights reserved. Used with permission.

EASTVILLE   SM

Unison

FRANCONIA   SM

1   Christ bids us break the bread
    and share the cup he gave,
    in token of the blood he shed
    for those he died to save.

2   It was for us he came,
    to bear, by human birth,
    a crown of thorn, a cross of shame,
    for every child of earth.

3   The Saviour crucified
    in glory rose again:
    we here remember him who died,
    ascended now to reign.

4   Our hearts his word obey,
    in thankfulness and love:
    we feed on Christ by faith today
    and feast with him above.

5   O Christ, once lifted up
    that we might be forgiven,
    we take the bread and drink the cup
    and share the life of heaven.

TIMOTHY DUDLEY-SMITH (*b.* 1926)

Music: 1: KENNETH NAYLOR (1931–1991)
Music: 2: J.B. König's *Harmonischer Lieder-Schatz,* Frankfurt, 1738
    Adapted by WILLIAM HENRY HAVERGAL (1793–1870)

ST BOTOLPH (Slater)   CM

ST STEPHEN (NEWINGTON)   CM

1   I come with joy, a child of God,
        forgiven, loved and free,
    the life of Jesus to recall,
        in love laid down for me.

2   I come with Christians far and near
        to find, as all are fed,
    the new community of love
        in Christ's communion bread.

3   As Christ breaks bread, and bids us share,
        each proud division ends.
    The love that made us, makes us one,
        and strangers now are friends.

4   The Spirit of the risen Christ,
        unseen, but ever near,
    is in such friendship better known,
        alive among us here.

5   Together met, together bound
        by all that God has done,
    we'll go with joy, to give the world
        the love that makes us one.

                                    BRIAN WREN (b.1936)

Music: 1: GORDON SLATER (1896–1979)
Music: 2: WILLIAM JONES (1726–1800)

JESUS CALLS US (LEWIS FOLK MELODY) 87 87 D

1 Jesus calls us here to meet him
    as, through word and song and prayer,
we affirm God's promised presence
    where his people live and care.
Praise the God who keeps his promise;
    praise the Son who calls us friends;
praise the Spirit who, among us,
    to our hopes and fears attends.

2 Jesus calls us to confess him
    Word of life and Lord of all,
sharer of our flesh and frailness,
    saving all who fail or fall.
Tell his holy human story;
    tell his tales that all may hear;
tell the world that Christ in glory
    came to earth to meet us here.

3 Jesus calls us to each other,
    vastly different though we are;
creed and colour, class and gender
    neither limit nor debar.
Join the hand of friend and stranger;
    join the hands of age and youth;
join the faithful and the doubter
    in their common search for truth.

Music: Lewis folk melody
    arranged by JOHN L. BELL (b. 1949)

218 Words: From *Love From Below,* 1989. © 1989, Wild Goose Resource Group, The Iona Community, 4th Floor, Savoy Centre, 140 Sauchiehall Street, Glasgow G2 3DH

* 4   Jesus calls us to his table
rooted firm in time and space,
where the Church in earth and heaven
finds a common meeting place.
Share the bread and wine, his body;
share the love of which we sing;
share the feast of saints and sinners
hosted by our Lord and King.

JOHN L. BELL (*b.*1949)
and GRAHAM MAULE (*b.*1958)

Verse 4 may be omitted when there is no celebration of Holy Communion.

219

CRESSWELL   88 97 and refrain

1   Love is his word, love is his way,
feasting with all, fasting alone,
living and dying, rising again;
love, only love, is his way.

Richer than gold is the love of my Lord,
better than splendour and wealth.

2   Love is his way, love is his mark,
sharing his last Passover feast,
Christ at the table, host to the twelve;
love, only love, is his mark.

Continued overleaf

Music: ANTHONY MILNER (1925–2002)

219   Words and Music: © McCrimmon Publishing Company Limited, 10-12 High Street, Great Wakering, Essex SS3 0EQ.
Used by permission.

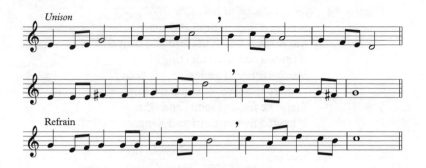

Unison

Refrain

3   Love is his mark, love is his sign,
    bread for our strength, wine for our joy,
    'This is my body, this is my blood.'
    Love, only love, is his sign.

    Richer than gold is the love of my Lord,
    better than splendour and wealth.

4   Love is his sign, love is his news,
    'Do this,' he said, 'lest you forget
    all my deep sorrow, all my dear blood.'
    Love, only love, is his news.

5   Love is his news, love is his name,
    we are his own, chosen and called,
    sisters and brothers, parents and kin.
    Love, only love, is his name.

6   Love is his name, love is his law,
    hear his command, all who are his:
    'Love one another; I have loved you.'
    Love, only love, is his law.

7   Love is his law, love is his word:
    love of the Lord, Father and Word,
    love of the Spirit, God ever one;
    love, only love, is his word.

                    * LUKE CONNAUGHTON (1917–1979)

KILLIBEGS   LM

SOLOTHURN   LM

1   Now let us from this table rise
       renewed in body, mind and soul;
     with Christ we die and rise again,
       his selfless love has made us whole.

2   With minds alert, upheld by grace,
       to spread the word in speech and deed,
     we follow in the steps of Christ,
       at one with all in hope and need.

3   To fill each human house with love,
       it is the sacrament of care;
     the work that Christ began to do
       we humbly pledge ourselves to share.

4   Then grant us grace, Companion-God,
       to choose again the pilgrim way
     and help us to accept with joy
       the challenge of tomorrow's day.

FRED KAAN (1929–2009)

Music: 1: WILLIAM DAVIES (*b.* 1921)

Music: 2: Swiss traditional melody in Reichart's *Frohe Lieder für deutsche Männer,* 1781, *arranged by* Compilers of *Common Praise,* 2000

Refrain

One bread,___ one bo-dy,_____ one Lord of all,

one cup of bless - ing which we bless.___ And

we,___ though ma-ny,_____ through-out the earth,

we are one bo-dy in this one Lord.___

To verses   *Last time*

1 Gen-tile or Jew,   ser-vant or free,

D.C

wo-man or man,___ no more.___

One bread, one body, one Lord of all,
one cup of blessing which we bless.
And we, though many, throughout the earth,
we are one body in this one Lord.

1   Gentile or Jew,
      servant or free,
      woman or man, no more.

2   Many the gifts,
      many the works,
      one in the Lord of all.

3   Grain for the fields,
      scattered and grown,
      gathered to one, for all.

JOHN FOLEY, SJ   (b. 1939)

Music: JOHN FOLEY , SJ (b. 1939)

BEACON HILL   10 10 10 10

1   The Lord is here — he finds us as we seek
      to learn his will and follow in his way.
      He gives himself just as he gave his Word,
      the God of promise greets us every day.

2   The Lord is here — he meets us as we share —
      this is the life he calls us now to live;
      in offered peace, in shared-out bread and wine,
      our God is gift and calls us now to give.

3   The Lord is here — inviting us to go
      and share the news with people everywhere.
      He waits outside in need and help alike,
      the Spirit moves through deed as well as prayer.

4   So let us go, intent to seek and find,
      living this hope that God is always near.
      Sharing and trusting, let us live his love,
      that all the world may say — 'The Lord is here.'

CHRISTOPHER J. ELLIS   (*b.* 1949)

Music: PETER WHITE (*b.* 1937)

MELANIE

66 66 88

1 The love of God comes close ___ where stands ___ an o - pen door   to let the stran - ger in, ___ to min - gle rich and poor: the love of God is here to stay, em - brac - ing those ___ who ___ walk his way.

Music: JOHN L. BELL (b. 1949)

1   The love of God comes close
    where stands an open door
    to let the stranger in,
    to mingle rich and poor:
    the love of God is here to stay,
    embracing those who walk his way.

2   The peace of God comes close
    to those caught in the storm,
    forgoing lives of ease
    to ease the lives forlorn:
    the peace of God is here to stay,
    embracing those who walk his way.

3   The joy of God comes close
    where faith encounters fears,
    where heights and depths of life
    are found through smiles and tears:
    the joy of God is here to stay,
    embracing those who walk his way.

4   The grace of God comes close
    to those whose grace is spent,
    when hearts are tired or sore
    and hope is bruised or bent:
    the grace of God is here to stay,
    embracing those who walk his way.

5   The Son of God comes close
    where people praise his name,
    where bread and wine are blest
    and shared, as when he came:
    the Son of God is here to stay,
    embracing those who walk his way.

JOHN L. BELL (b. 1949)
and GRAHAM MAULE (b. 1958)

223 Words and Music: From *Enemy of Apathy*, 1988. © 1988, Wild Goose Resource Group, The Iona Community, 4th Floor, Savoy Centre, 140 Sauchiehall Street, Glasgow G2 3DH

NICOLAUS (LOBT GOTT IHR CHRISTEN)   86 88 6

1.   All glory be to God on high,
his peace on earth proclaim;
to all his people tell abroad
the grace and glory of the Lord,
and bless his holy name.

2.   In songs of thankfulness and praise
our hearts their homage bring
to worship him who reigns above,
almighty Father, Lord of love,
our God and heavenly King.

3.   O Christ, the Father's only Son,
O Lamb enthroned on high,
O Jesus, who for sinners died
and reigns at God the Father's side,
in mercy hear our cry.

4.   Most high and holy is the Lord,
most high his heavenly throne;
where God the Father, God the Son,
and God the Spirit, ever One,
in glory reigns alone.

TIMOTHY DUDLEY-SMITH (b. 1926)
based on *Gloria in excelsis*

Music: NIKOLAUS HERMANN (1500–1561)
arranged by JOHANN SEBASTIAN BACH (1685–1750)

HEBRIDEAN GLORIA

Refrain

Glo - ri - a, glo - ri - a in ex - cel - sis, in ex - cel - sis. Glo - ri - a, glo - ri - a in ex - cel - sis De - - o.

1 Peace on earth to all your peo - ple, Lord God, heav'n - ly King. We wor - ship you, al - migh - ty Fa - ther, let our voi - ces ring! Sing:

2 Jesus, blessèd Lamb of God,
to you our voice we raise.
You take away our sins, O Lord,
receive our song of praise! Sing:

3 Holy Lord in highest heaven,
how our hearts rejoice
in God the Father, Son and Spirit,
so with loudest voice sing:

BARBARA RUSBRIDGE (b. 1953)
based on *Gloria in excelsis*

'*Gloria in excelsis Deo*' — '*Glory to God in the highest.*'

Music: Hebridean folk melody
arranged by BARBARA RUSBRIDGE (b. 1953)

LAND OF REST

Holy, holy, holy Lord,
God of power and might,
heaven and earth are full of your glory.
Hosanna in the highest.

Blessed is he who comes
in the name of the Lord.
Hosanna in the highest.
Hosanna in the highest.

Liturgical text

Music: American traditional melody
adapted by GEOFF WEAVER (*b.* 1943)

Holy, holy, holy is the Lord God almighty.
Holy, holy, holy is the Lord God almighty,
who was and is and is to come,
who was and is and is to come.

Lift up his name with the sound of singing,
lift up his name in all the earth.
Lift up your voice and give him glory,
for he is worthy to be praised.

NATHAN FELLINGHAM (*b.* 1977)

Music: NATHAN FELLINGHAM (*b.* 1977)

AGNUS DEI (St Bride)

Cantor *Slowly*

Lamb of God, you take a-way the sin of the world,

All

Lamb of God, you take a-way the sin of the

have_ mer-cy, on us. Lamb of God, you take a-way the

world, have_ mer-cy on us. Lamb of God, you

sin of the world, have_ mer-cy, on us.

take a-way the sin of the world, have_ mer-cy

Lamb of God, you take a-way the sin of the

on us. Lamb of God, you take a-way the

world, grant_ us your peace, grant_ us your

sin of the world, grant_ us your peace,

peace, grant_ us your peace._____

grant_ us your peace, grant_ us your peace.

Lamb of God,
you take away the sin of the world,
have mercy on us.

Lamb of God,
you take away the sin of the world,
have mercy on us.

Lamb of God,
you take away the sin of the world,
grant us your peace,
grant us your peace,
grant us your peace.

Liturgical text

Music: JOHN L. BELL (*b.* 1949)

228 Music: From *Come All You People*, 1995. © 1995, Wild Goose Resource Group,
The Iona Community, 4th Floor, Savoy Centre, 140 Sauchiehall Street, Glasgow G2 3DH

The refrain may be sung as an ostinato, omitting the verses.
The verses may be sung by one or more voices (between repetitions of the refrain)
while the accompanying chords are played or hummed.

Music: JACQUES BERTHIER (1923–1994)

Cantor or group

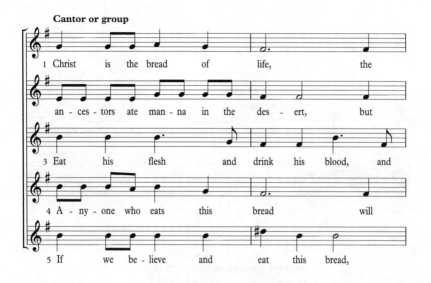

1 Christ is the bread of life, the
an - ces - tors ate man - na in the des - ert, but
3 Eat his flesh and drink his blood, and
4 A - ny - one who eats this bread will
5 If we be - lieve and eat this bread,

D.C.

true bread sent from the Fa - ther.
this is the bread come down from heav - en.
Christ will raise you up on the last day.
live for ev - - er.
we will have e - ter - nal life.

Taizé Community
based on John 6

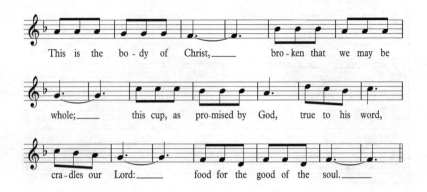

This is the body of Christ,
broken that we may be whole;
this cup, as promised by God,
true to his word, cradles our Lord:
food for the good of the soul.

JOHN L. BELL (b. 1949)

Music: JOHN L. BELL (b. 1949)

230 Words and Music: From *There Is One Among Us*, 1998. © 1998, Wild Goose Resource Group,
The Iona Community, 4th Floor, Savoy Centre, 140 Sauchiehall Street, Glasgow G2 3DH

SENDING

Briskly

Sent by the Lord am I; my hands are rea-dy now to

make the earth the place in which the king-dom comes. Sent

by the Lord am I; my hands are rea-dy now to

make the earth the place in which the king-dom comes. The

an-gels can-not change a world of hurt and pain in-

to a world of love, of jus-tice and of peace. The

task is mine to do, to set it real-ly free. Oh,

help me to o-bey; help me to do your will.

JORGE MALDONADO

Music: Central American folk melody
arranged by JOHN L. BELL (*b.* 1949)

231 Words: © 1991 Jorge Maldonado. Permission applied for.

231 Arrangement: From *Sent By The Lord*, 1991. © 1991, Wild Goose Resource Group,
The Iona Community, 4th Floor, Savoy Centre, 140 Sauchiehall Street, Glasgow G2 3DH

You shall go out with joy___ and be led forth with peace,_
_ and the moun-tains and the hills shall break forth be -
- fore you. There'll be shouts of joy___ and the trees of the
field shall___ clap, shall clap their hands,
and the trees of the field shall clap their hands,_
_ and the trees of the field shall clap their hands,_
_ and the trees of the field shall clap their hands,_
_ and you'll go out with joy.___

STUART DAUERMANN (*b.*1944)
based on Isaiah 55.12

Music: STUART DAUERMANN (*b.*1944)
    arranged by ANTHONY F. CARVER (*b.*1947) and ANNE HARRISON (*b.*1954)

CELTIC ALLELUIA

Now with the strength of your Word, send us to be your di-
sci - ples to bring all the world to the
joy of your King - dom.

FINTAN O'CARROLL (1922–1981)
and CHRISTOPHER WALKER (b. 1947)

Music: FINTAN O'CARROLL (1922–1981) and CHRISTOPHER WALKER (b. 1947)

THUMA MINA

Cantor:

1   Send me, Lord.

All:

Send me, Jesus, send me, Jesus,
send me, Jesus, send me, Lord.

Cantor:

2   Lead me, Lord.

All:

Lead me, Jesus, lead me, Jesus,
lead me, Jesus, lead me, Lord.

Cantor:

3   Fill me, Lord.

All:

Fill me, Jesus, fill me, Jesus,
fill me, Jesus, fill me, Lord.

Original Xhosa text:
Cantor:
Thuma mina.
All:
Thuma mina, thuma mina,
thuma mina, Somandla.

South African traditional
adapted by ANDERS NYBERG   (b. 1955)

Music: South African traditional hymn
adapted by ANDERS NYBERG (b. 1955)

SIYAHAMBA

We are marching in the light of God,
we are marching in the light of God.
We are marching in the light of God,
we are marching in the light of God.
We are marching, oh,
we are marching in the light of God.
We are marching, oh,
we are marching in the light of God.

Original Xhosa text:
Siyahamb' ekukhanyen' kwenkhos'

Xhosa (South African) traditional hymn
adapted by ANDERS NYBERG (*b.* 1955)

Music: South African traditional melody
arranged by ANDERS NYBERG (*b.* 1955)

235 Words and Music: From *Freedom Is Coming*, 1990. © 1990, Wild Goose Resource Group,
The Iona Community, 4th Floor, Savoy Centre, 140 Sauchiehall Street, Glasgow G2 3DH

GOD and the WORLD

Al - le - lu - ia!   Al - le - lu - ia!   Raise the Gos - pel

o - ver the earth!_   Al - le - lu - ia!   Al - le - lu - ia!

Fine

Peace   and   jus - - tice   bring - ing   to   birth!_

1 Bless - ed   those whose hearts are   gen - tle.   Bless - ed   those whose
2 Bless - ed   those   who work   for   jus - tice.   Bless - ed   those who
3 Trem - ble,   you   who build   up   rich - es.   Trem - ble,   you   with
4 Trem - ble,   you   who thirst   for   pow - er.   Trem - ble,   you who
5 Glo - ry   like   the   stars   of   hea - ven.   Glo - ry   like   the
6 Glo - ry   to   the   Word   of   Jus - tice.   Glo - ry   to   the

(1) spi - rits are strong._   Bless - ed   those who choose   to   bring forth
(2) an - swer the call.__   Bless - ed   those who dare   to   dream of
(3) op - u - lent lives.__   Trem - ble,   when you meet   the   poor and
(4) live for ac - claim.__   Trem - ble,   when you find   no   com - fort
(5) sun   in   the sky.__   Glo - ry   shines up - on   all   peo - ple,
(6) Spi - rit of Peace.__   Glo - ry   to   the   God   of   Love whose

D.C.

(1) right   where   there   is   wrong.
(2) last - - ing   peace   for   all.
(3) see   Christ   in   their   eyes.
(4) in   your   wealth   and   fame.
(5) e - - qual   in   God's   eyes.
(6) bless - - ings   nev - - er   cease.

Music: BERNADETTE FARRELL (*b.* 1957)

Alleluia! Alleluia!
Raise the Gospel over the earth!
Alleluia! Alleluia!
Peace and justice bringing to birth!

1   Blessed those whose hearts are gentle.
    Blessed those whose spirits are strong.
    Blessed those who choose to bring forth
        right where there is wrong.

2   Blessed those who work for justice.
    Blessed those who answer the call.
    Blessed those who dare to dream
        of lasting peace for all.

3   Tremble, you who build up riches.
    Tremble, you with opulent lives.
    Tremble, when you meet the poor
        and see Christ in their eyes.

4   Tremble, you who thirst for power.
    Tremble, you who live for acclaim.
    Tremble, when you find no comfort
        in your wealth and fame.

5   Glory like the stars of heaven.
    Glory like the sun in the sky.
    Glory shines upon all people,
        equal in God's eyes.

6   Glory to the Word of Justice.
    Glory to the Spirit of Peace.
    Glory to the God of Love
        whose blessings never cease.

OWEN ALSTOTT (*b.* 1947)

1 Beau - ty for bro - ken-ness, hope for des - pair,
3 Re - fuge from cru - el wars, ha - vens from fear,

Lord, in your suf - fering world this is our prayer.
ci - ties for sanc - tu - ary, free - doms to share.

Bread for the child - ren, just - ice, joy, peace,
Peace to the kill - ing fields, scorched earth to green,

sun - rise to sun - set your king - dom in - crease!
Christ for the bit - ter - ness, his cross for the pain.

2 Shel - ter for
4 Rest for the
5 Light - en our

fra - gile lives, cures for their ills, work for the
ra - vaged earth, o - ceans and streams, plun - dered and
dark - ness, breathe on this flame, un - til your

crafts - men, trade for their skills. Land for the
poi - soned: our fu - ture, our dreams. Lord, end our
jus - tice burns bright - ly a - gain; un - til the

Music: **GRAHAM KENDRICK** (*b.* 1950)
    arranged by **JOHN BARNARD** (*b.* 1948)

GOD AND THE WORLD

dis - pos-sessed,   rights   for   the   weak,   voi - ces   to
mad - ness,   care - less - ness,   greed;   make   us   con -
na - tions   learn   of   your   ways,   seek   your   sal -

plead the cause   of   those   who   can't   speak.   *God   of   the   poor,*
tent__ with   the   things   that   we   need.
va - tion   and   bring   you   their   praise.

Refrain

friend   of   the   weak,__   give   us   com - pas -

- - sion,   we   pray: melt   our   cold   hearts,   let

tears   fall   like__   rain.   Come,   change   our   love__   from   a

1st time   2nd time   D.S.

spark_____   to   a__   flame.   flame.

Last time

flame.

GRAHAM KENDRICK (b. 1950)

237 Words and Music: © 1993, Graham Kendrick / Make Way Music Ltd, PO Box 320, Tunbridge Wells, Kent. TN2 9DE UK. <www.grahamkendrick.co.uk> Used by permission.

BLACKBIRD LEYS   10 10 10 10

1   Creating God, we bring our song of praise
       for life and work that celebrate your ways:
           the skill of hands, our living with the earth,
           the joy that comes from knowing our own worth.

2   Forgiving God, we bring our cries of pain
       for all that shames us in our search for gain:
           the hidden wounds, the angry scars of strife,
           the emptiness that saps and weakens life.

3   Redeeming God, we bring our trust in you,
       our fragile hope that all may be made new:
           our dreams of truth, of wealth that all may share,
           of work and service rooted deep in prayer.

4   Renewing God, we offer what shall be
       a world that lives and works in harmony:
           when peace and justice, once so long denied,
           restore to all their dignity and pride.

JAN BERRY   (b. 1953)

Music: PETER CUTTS (b. 1937)

MELITA 88 88 88

1   Creator God, the world around
        declares your glory — flower and tree,
    the evening sky and torrent's sound
        and mountain stream and rolling sea.
    Yet all this beauty cannot show
    a God whom we can truly know.

2   Composer God, all music sings
        your power, your praise, your majesty:
    in drum and trumpet, flute and strings,
        in choir and song and symphony.
    Yet music which inspires our praise
    can never fathom all your ways.

3   Designer God, in shape and form
        the beauty you inspire is shown;
    in line and colour, etched or drawn,
        in sculpture, painting, glass and stone.
    Yet all these talents can't express
    the full truth of your loveliness.

4   Mysterious God, though all the arts
        of nature and of human skill
    may move us, yet our longing hearts
        are never satisfied until
    in Jesus Christ you show your face:
    a God of love and truth and grace.

BRIAN HOARE (*b.* 1935)

Music: JOHN BACCHUS DYKES (1823–1876)

FREE INDEED   14 14 14 and refrain

1   Cry 'Freedom!' in the name of God, and let the cry resound;
     proclaim for all that freedom which in Jesus Christ is found,
     for none of us is truly free while anyone is bound.

     Cry 'Freedom!' Cry 'Freedom!'
     Cry 'Freedom!' in God's name!

2   Cry 'Freedom!' for the victims of the earthquake and the rain:
     where wealthy folk find shelter and the poor must bear the pain;
     where weapons claim resources while the famine strikes again.

3   Cry 'Freedom!' for dictators in their fortresses confined,
     who hide behind their bodyguards and fear the open mind,
     and bid them find true freedom in the good of humankind.

4   Cry 'Freedom!' in the church when honest doubts are met with fear;
     when vacuum-packed theology makes questions disappear;
     when journeys end before they start and mystery is clear!

5   Cry 'Freedom!' when we find ourselves imprisoned in our greed,
     to live in free relationship and meet each other's need.
     From self released for others' good we should be free indeed!

                                        MICHAEL FORSTER (*b.* 1946)

Music: PETER NARDONE (*b.* 1965)

KING'S LYNN   76 76 D
Unison

1   Extol the God of justice
     with heart and soul and voice;
   remember all his wonders,
     recount them and rejoice.
   He stands with all who labour
     for what is true and right,
   till wickedness and falsehood
     are banished from his sight.

2   Extol the God of justice
     enthroned for evermore,
   a stronghold in affliction,
     a refuge to the poor:
   he hears the cry of victims
     and senses their despair;
   in faithfulness he honours
     the faith that sparks our prayer.

3   Extol the God of justice,
     however dark the day:
   the hope that calls for mercy
     will not be turned away;
   for evil shall not triumph,
     nor human sin prevail:
   the Lord is God eternal,
     whose judgements cannot fail.

MARTIN LECKEBUSCH (*b.* 1962)
based on Psalm 9

Music: English traditional melody
collected and arranged by RALPH VAUGHAN WILLIAMS (1872–1958)

PICARDY   87 87 87

1   God of freedom, God of justice,
     God whose love is strong as death,
     God who saw the dark of prison,
     God who knew the price of faith:
         touch our world of sad oppression
         with your Spirit's healing breath.

2   Rid the earth of torture's terror,
     God whose hands were nailed to wood;
     hear the cries of pain and protest,
     God who shed both tears and blood;
         move in us the power of pity,
         restless for the common good.

3   Make in us a captive conscience
     quick to hear, to act, to plead;
     make us truly sisters, brothers
     of whatever race or creed:
         teach us to be fully human,
         open to each other's need.

                    SHIRLEY ERENA MURRAY (b. 1931) (alt.)

Music: French carol melody
     harmonised by RALPH VAUGHAN WILLIAMS (1872–1958)

RHUDDLAN 87 87 87

1 Gracious God, in adoration
    saints with joy before you fall;
    only when our hearts are leaden
    can we fail to hear their call:
    'Come with wonder, serve with gladness
    God whose power created all.'

2 Earth and sky in silent praises
    speak to those with eyes to see;
    all earth's living creatures echo
    'God has made us!' So may we
    come with wonder, serve with gladness
    him through whom they came to be.

3 You have made us in your image,
    breathed your Spirit, giv'n us birth;
    Jesus calls, whose cross has given
    every life eternal worth,
    'Come with wonder, serve with gladness,
    let God's will be done on earth!'

4 Earth by war and want is threatened;
    deep the roots of fear and greed;
    let your mercy be our measure
    as we see our neighbour's need,
    come with wonder, serve with gladness,
    share your gift of daily bread.

5 Holy Spirit, urging, striving,
    give us love that casts out fear,
    courage, seeking peace with justice,
    faith to make this message clear —
    'Come with wonder, serve with gladness,
    live in hope; the Lord is near!'

BASIL BRIDGE (b. 1927)

Music: Welsh traditional melody in *Musical Relics of Welsh Bards,* 1800
harmonised by Compilers of *English Hymnal,* 1906

HARESFIELD CM

1 How good it is, what pleasure comes,
      when people live as one.
   When peace and justice light the way
      the will of God is done.

2 True friendship then like fragrant oil
      surrounds us with delight;
   and blessings shine like morning dew
      upon the mountain height.

3 How good it is when walls of fear
      come tumbling to the ground.
   When arms are changed to farming tools
      the fruits of life abound.

4 What quiet joy can bloom and grow
      when people work for peace,
   when hands and voices join as one
      that hate and war may cease.

RUTH C. DUCK (b. 1947)
based on Psalm 133

Music: JOHN DYKES BOWER (1905–1981)

SALLEY GARDENS   76 76 D

1 Inspired by love and anger,
       disturbed by need and pain,
   informed of God's own bias,
       we ponder once again:
   'How long must some folk suffer?
       How long can few folk mind?
   How long dare vain self-interest
       turn prayer and pity blind?'

2 From those forever victims
       of heartless human greed,
   their cruel plight composes
       a litany of need:
   'Where are the fruits of justice?
       Where are the signs of peace?
   When is the day when prisoners
       and dreams find their release?'

*3 From those forever shackled
       to what their wealth can buy,
   the fear of lost advantage
       provokes the bitter cry,
   'Don't query our position!
       Don't criticize our wealth!
   Don't mention those exploited
       by politics and stealth!'

Continued overleaf

Music: Irish folk melody
   arranged by JOHN L. BELL (b. 1949)

245 Words: From *Heaven Shall Not Wait*, 1987. © 1987, Wild Goose Resource Group, The Iona Community, 4th Floor, Savoy Centre, 140 Sauchiehall Street, Glasgow G2 3DH

* 4 To God, who through the prophets
        proclaimed a different age,
    we offer earth's indifference,
        its agony and rage:
    'When will the wrongs be righted?
    When will the kingdom come?
    When will the world be generous
        to all instead of some?'

5   God asks, 'Who will go for me?
        Who will extend my reach?
    And who, when few will listen,
        will prophesy and preach?
    And who, when few bid welcome,
        will offer all they know?
    And who, when few dare follow,
        will walk the road I show?'

6   Amused in someone's kitchen,
        asleep in someone's boat,
    attuned to what the ancients
        exposed, proclaimed and wrote,
    a saviour without safety,
        a tradesman without tools
    has come to tip the balance
        with fishermen and fools.

JOHN L. BELL (b. 1949)
and GRAHAM MAULE (b. 1958)

NOEL NOUVELET   11 11 10 11

1   Jesus Christ is waiting, waiting in the streets:
      no one is his neighbour, all alone he eats.
      Listen, Lord Jesus, I am lonely too;
      make me, friend or stranger, fit to wait on you.

2   Jesus Christ is raging, raging in the streets,
      where injustice spirals and real hope retreats.
      Listen, Lord Jesus, I am angry too;
      in the Kingdom's causes let me rage with you.

3   Jesus Christ is healing, healing in the streets,
      curing those who suffer, touching those he greets.
      Listen, Lord Jesus, I have pity too;
      let my care be active, healing, just like you.

4   Jesus Christ is dancing, dancing in the streets,
      where each sign of hatred he, with love, defeats.
      Listen, Lord Jesus, I should triumph too;
      where good conquers evil, let me dance with you.

5   Jesus Christ is calling, calling in the streets,
      'Who will join my journey? I will guide their feet.'
      Listen, Lord Jesus, let my fears be few:
      walk one step before me, I will follow you.

JOHN L. BELL (*b.* 1949)
and GRAHAM MAULE (*b.* 1958)

Music: French carol
       harmonised by JOHN L. BELL (*b.* 1949)

246 Words: From *Enemy of Apathy,* 1988. © 1988, Wild Goose Resource Group,
The Iona Community, 4th Floor, Savoy Centre, 140 Sauchiehall Street, Glasgow G2 3DH

DARWALL'S 148th   66 66 44 44

1   Let all creation dance
       in energies sublime,
     as order turns with chance,
       unfolding space and time;
         for nature's art
         in glory grows,
         and newly shows
         God's mind and heart.

2   God's breath each force unfurls,
       igniting from a spark
     expanding starry swirls,
       with whirlpools dense and dark.
         Though moon and sun
         seem mindless things,
         each orbit sings:
         your will be done.

3   Our own amazing earth,
       with sunlight, cloud and storms,
     and life's abundant growth
       in lovely shapes and forms
         is made for praise,
         a fragile whole,
         and from its soul
         heaven's music plays.

4   Lift heart and soul and voice:
       in Christ all praises meet,
     and nature shall rejoice
       as all is made complete.

Music: JOHN DARWALL (1731–1789)

In hope be strong,
all life befriend,
and kindly tend
creation's song.

BRIAN WREN (b.1936)

248

INTERCESSOR   11 10 11 10

1   Lord of all worlds, we worship and adore you,
      creation sings a galaxy of praise:
    the planets fly, the stars cry out in wonder,
      new life appears, evolving in its ways.

2   You forged the sun, the molten light of morning;
      you scattered stars, flung jewels of the night;
    you are the day which penetrates our darkness:
      fill us with hope that we might share your light.

3   You summoned land from dark and heaving oceans,
      you moulded hills and carved the mountains high,
    you are the artist who is still creating:
      make us your partners lest the earth should die.

4   The glittering shoals flash through the rippling water,
      the gliding gull ascends the stream of air:
    now leaping thought and consecrated action
      become our way of living and of prayer.

5   You are the wind that rushes through the heavens,
      the breath that gently feeds us from our birth:
    we rest in you, our source and goal of living,
      we strive for you as stewards of your earth.

CHRISTOPHER J. ELLIS (b.1949)

Music: CHARLES HUBERT HASTINGS PARRY (1848–1918)

HOW GREAT THOU ART   11 10 11 10 and refrain

Then sings my soul, my Sa-viour God, to thee, 'How great thou art! How great thou art!' Then sings my soul, my Sa-viour God, to thee, 'How great thou art! How great thou art!'

Music: Swedish folk melody
  arranged by STUART HINE (1899–1989)

1   O Lord my God, when I in awesome wonder
      consider all the works thy hand hath made,
    I see the stars, I hear the mighty thunder,
      thy power throughout the universe displayed:

    Then sings my soul, my Saviour God to thee,
      'How great thou art! How great thou art!'
    Then sings my soul, my Saviour God to thee,
      'How great thou art! How great thou art!'

2   When through the woods and forest glades I wander
      and hear the birds sing sweetly in the trees;
    when I look down from lofty mountain grandeur,
      and hear the brook, and feel the gentle breeze:

3   And when I think that God, his Son not sparing,
      sent him to die, I scarce can take it in,
    that on the cross, my burden gladly bearing,
      he bled and died to take away my sin:

4   When Christ shall come with shout of acclamation
      and take me home — what joy shall fill my heart!
    Then shall I bow in humble adoration
      and there proclaim, 'My God, how great thou art!'

STUART HINE (1899–1989)
vv. 1, 2, 4 based on *O store Gud* 1885
by CARL GUSTAF BOBERG (1859–1940)

LIFE OF THE WORLD

1   Oh, the life of the world is a joy and a treasure,
    unfolding in beauty the green-growing tree,
    the changing of seasons in mountain and valley,
        the stars and the bright restless sea.

2   Oh, the life of the world is a fountain of goodness
    overflowing in labour and passion and pain,
    in the sound of the city and the silence of wisdom,
        in the birth of a child once again.

3   Oh, the life of the world is the source of our healing.
    It rises in laughter and wells up in song;
    it springs from the care of the poor and the broken
        and refreshes where justice is strong.

4   So give thanks for the life and give love to the Maker,
    and rejoice in the gift of the bright risen Son,
    and walk in the peace and the power of the Spirit
        till the days of our living are done.

KATHRYN GALLOWAY (b. 1952)

Music: Melody by IAN GALLOWAY (b. 1952)
    arranged by JOHN L. BELL (b. 1949)

ST COLUMBA (ERIN)   87 87

1   Put peace into each other's hands
    and like a treasure hold it,
    protect it like a candle-flame,
    with tenderness enfold it.

2   Put peace into each other's hands
    with loving expectation;
    be gentle in your words and ways,
    in touch with God's creation.

3   Put peace into each other's hands
    like bread we break for sharing;
    look people warmly in the eye:
    our life is meant for caring.

4   Give thanks for strong — yet tender — hands,
    held out in trust and blessing.
    Where words fall short, let hands speak out,
    the heights of love expressing.

5   Reach out in friendship, stay with faith
    in touch with those around you.
    Put peace into each other's hands:
    the Peace that sought and found you.

                          FRED KAAN (1929–2009)

Music: Petrie *Collection of Irish Melody*
    harmonised by Compilers of Irish *Church Hymnal,* 1874

PLEADING SAVIOUR (SALTASH)   87 87 D

Music: Melody from Henry Ward Beecher: *Plymouth collection of hymns and tunes,* New York, 1855 *arranged by* RALPH VAUGHAN WILLIAMS (1872–1958)

1   Sing the gospel of salvation,
       tell it out to all the earth;
   to the ones so long excluded,
       speak of hope and human worth.
   All the darkness of injustice
       cannot dim salvation's light,
   for the outcast and exploited
       count as worthy in God's sight.

2   Christ, the one eternal Shepherd,
       calls creation to rejoice,
   and the victims of oppression
       thrill to hear salvation's voice.
   All who recognize the Saviour
       take their place within the fold,
   there, in perfect truth and freedom,
       life's eternal joys to hold.

3   See, the host that none can number
       gathers in from every side,
   once the victims of injustice,
       now redeemed and glorified.
   Fear and weeping here are ended,
       hunger and oppression cease.
   Now the Lamb becomes the Shepherd!
       Now begins the reign of peace!

MICHAEL FORSTER (b. 1946)

252 Words: © 1993, Kevin Mayhew Ltd, Buxhall, Stowmarket, Suffolk IP14 3BW Used by permission.

RADCLIFFE SQUARE   10 10 10 10

4 Take up the song, and sing the praise of
God; with music make both earth and heaven
ring, for God is good and loves all he has
made; so now to him all thanks and praises bring!

Music: GEOFFREY WEBBER (*b.* 1959)

1 Take up the song, and sing the praise of God,
   who gave the world its skies and lands and seas,
   then formed the fish and creatures of the earth;
   our God be praised for wondrous gifts like these!

2 Take up the song, and sing the praise of God,
   who gave the power of choice to humankind,
   that we might rule the earth through servanthood,
   and so find joy in all that God designed.

3 Take up the song, and sing the praise of God;
   proclaim to all the open mystery
   that Christ, whose death destroyed the power of sin,
   was raised by God and reigns in Trinity.

4 Take up the song, and sing the praise of God;
   with music make both earth and heaven ring,
   for God is good and loves all he has made;
   so now to him all thanks and praises bring!

RAE E. WHITNEY (b. 1927)

PADERBORN   10 10 11 11

1   The kingdom of God is justice and joy,
     for Jesus restores what sin would destroy;
    God's power and glory in Jesus we know,
     and here and hereafter the kingdom shall grow.

2   The kingdom of God is mercy and grace,
     the captives are freed, the sinners find place,
     the outcast are welcomed God's banquet to share,
     and hope is awakened instead of despair.

3   The kingdom of God is challenge and choice,
     believe the good news, repent and rejoice!
    His love for us sinners brought Christ to his cross,
     our crisis of judgement for gain or for loss.

4   God's kingdom is come, the gift and the goal,
     in Jesus begun, in heaven made whole;
     the heirs of the kingdom shall answer his call,
     and all things cry 'Glory!' to God all in all.

* BRYN REES (1911–1983)

Music: German folk melody included in *Gesangbuch*, Paderborn, 1765
     arranged by SYDNEY HUGO NICHOLSON (1875–1947)

255

BUGEILIO'R GWENITH GWYN   87 87 D

GOD AND THE WORLD

1 To you, O Christ, the Prince of Peace,
   the source of love and pity,
we bring in prayer and penitence
   the countryside and city;
the poverty that troubles both,
   the vanity that fools us,
the walls that keep our lives apart,
   the ignorance that rules us.

2 As once you walked in Galilee
   and learned its paths and valleys,
or met within Jerusalem
   the crowds from streets and alleys;
so help us learn our age's needs
   and meet those needs with caring,
your world and people see in all,
   your love and gospel sharing.

3 Lord, let us never pass our days
   indifferent to others;
or build up walls that hide from sight
   our sisters and our brothers;
through windows barred and shuttered tight
   how can your sunshine reach us?
O make us open to your truth,
   your love and service teach us.

4 May all the darkness we have made
   and sins that have controlled us
fade in the glory of your light,
   and your strong love enfold us.
Bring us to new Jerusalem,
   your Bride from heaven descending,
the City of the Father's peace
   and joy that has no ending.

RICHARD STURCH (b. 1936)

Music: Welsh 18th-century folksong
   arranged by JOHN BARNARD (b. 1948)

255 Words: © 1991, Stainer & Bell Ltd, 23 Gruneisen Road, London N3 1DZ <www.stainer.co.uk>

ST PATRICK'S BREASTPLATE   DLM

1.   We do not hope to ease our minds
     by simple answers, shifted blame,
    while Christ is homeless, hungry, poor,
     and we are rich who bear his name.
    As long as justice is a dream
     and human dignity denied,
    we stand with Christ; disturb us still
     till every need is satisfied.

2.   We cannot ask to live at peace
     in comfort and security
    while Christ is tried in Pilate's hall
     and drags his cross to Calvary.
    As long as hatred stifles truth
     and freedom is betrayed by fear,
    we stand with Christ; give us no peace
     till his peace reigns in triumph here.

Music: Irish traditional melody
     arranged by CHARLES VILLIERS STANFORD (1852–1924)

3   We will not pray to be preserved
       from any depths of agony
    while Christ's despairing cry rings out:
       God, why have you abandoned me?
    As long as we have hope to share
       of life renewed beyond the pain,
    we stand with Christ all through the night
       till Easter morning dawns again.

MARNIE BARRELL *(b. 1952)*

257

THIS ENDRIS NYGHT   CM

1   We sing your praise, eternal God,
       to whom all praise belongs;
    but we can never match your love,
       however loud our songs:

2   Your love which comes so silently,
       through all the noise we hear;
    the noise of quarrelling and war
       the cries of grief and fear.

3   The winds of doubt uproot our faith,
       the earthquakes of despair
    destroy our hope, and fires of hate
       kill love and stifle prayer.

4   And yet no sound on earth can drown
       the silence we have heard;
    the voice of your eternal love;
       the silence of your Word.

5   It comes to guilty, broken hearts,
       with challenge and release;
    prepares us for self-sacrifice
       and speaks eternal peace.

ALAN GAUNT *(b. 1935)*

Music: English 15th-century carol

1 Who can sound the depths of sorrow
  in the father-heart of God,
 for the children we've rejected,
  for the lives so deeply scarred?
 And each light that we've extinguished
  has brought darkness to our land:
 upon our nation, upon our nation
  have mercy, Lord!

Music: GRAHAM KENDRICK (*b.* 1950)

2   We have scorned the truth you gave us,
     we have bowed to other lords,
   we have sacrificed the children
     on the altars of our gods.
   O let truth again shine on us,
     let your holy fear descend:
   upon our nation, upon our nation
     have mercy, Lord!

3   Who can stand before your anger?
     Who can face your piercing eyes?
   For you love the weak and helpless,
     and you hear the victims' cries.
   Yes, you are a God of justice
     and your judgement surely comes:
   upon our nation, upon our nation
     have mercy, Lord!

4   Who will stand against the violence?
     Who will comfort those who mourn?
   In an age of cruel rejection,
     who will build for love a home?
   Come and shake us into action,
     come and melt our hearts of stone:
   upon your people, upon your people
     have mercy, Lord!

5   Who can sound the depths of mercy
     in the father-heart of God?
   For there is a Man of sorrows
     who for sinners shed his blood.
   He can heal the wounds of nations,
     he can wash the guilty clean:
   because of Jesus, because of Jesus,
     have mercy, Lord!

GRAHAM KENDRICK (b. 1950)

258 Words and Music: © 1988, Graham Kendrick / Make Way Music Ltd, PO Box 320, Tunbridge Wells, Kent. TN2 9DE UK. <www.grahamkendrick.co.uk> Used by permission.

GENERAL

1 As the deer pants___ for the wa - ter, so my
2 I want you more than gold or sil - ver, on - ly
3 You're my Friend and___ you're my Bro - ther, e - ven

soul longs af - - ter you. You a - lone are my
you can sa - - tis - fy. You a - lone are the
though you are a king. I love you more than

heart's de - sire,___ and I long to wor - ship you.
real joy - giv - er and the ap - - ple of my eye.
a - ny oth - er, so much more than a - - ny - thing.

Refrain, Harmony

You a - lone are my strength, my shield, to you a -

- lone may my spi - rit yield. You a - lone are my

heart's de - sire,___ and I long to wor - ship you.

MARTIN J. NYSTROM   (*b.* 1956)

Music: MARTIN J. NYSTROM (*b.* 1956)
adapted by Compilers of *Church Hymnary,* 4th edition, 2005

260

Meditatively

v. 4

1 Be - cause the Lord is my

shep - herd,___ I have ev - ery - thing___ I need. He lets me

rest in the meadow and leads me____ to the qui-et streams. He re-

-stores_ my soul and he leads me____ in the paths that are right:

Refrain

Lord, you are my shepherd, you are my friend. I want to fol-low you

vv. 1, 2, 3

al-ways, just to fol-low my friend. 2 And

v. 4

friend.

2 And when the road leads to darkness,
   I shall walk there unafraid.
   Even when death is close I have courage,
   for your help is there.
   You are close beside me with comfort,
   you are guiding my way:

3 In love you make me a banquet
   for my enemies to see.
   You make me welcome,
   pouring down honour from your mighty hand,
   and this joy fills me with gladness;
   it is too much to bear:

4 Your goodness always is with me
   and your mercy I know.
   Your loving kindness strengthens me always
   as I go through life.
   I shall dwell in your presence for ever,
   giving praise to your name:

CHRISTOPHER WALKER (b. 1947)
based on Psalm 23, *Living Bible* version

Music: CHRISTOPHER WALKER (b. 1947)

BEFORE THE THRONE OF GOD   DLM extended

1 Be-fore the throne of God a-bove I have a strong, a per-fect plea, a great High Priest, whose name is Love, who ev-er lives and pleads for me. My name is gra-ven on his hands, my name is writ-ten on his heart; I know that while in heaven he stands no tongue can bid me thence de-part, no tongue can bid me thence de-part.

2   When Satan tempts me to despair,
     and tells me of the guilt within,
upward I look, and see him there
     who made an end of all my sin.
Because the sinless Saviour died,
     my sinful soul is counted free;
for God, the Just, is satisfied
     to look on him and pardon me,
     to look on him and pardon me.

3   Behold him there! the risen Lamb!
     my perfect, spotless Righteousness,
the great unchangeable I AM,
     the King of glory and of grace!
One with my Lord, I cannot die;
     my soul is purchased by his blood;
my life is hid with Christ on high,
     with Christ, my Saviour and my God,
     with Christ, my Saviour and my God.

        * CHARITIE L. DE CHENEZ (1841–1923)

Music: VIKKI COOK

261 Music: © 1997 Sovereign Grace Music / Integrity's Hosanna! Music / Integrity Music Europe, PO Box 39, Westham, BN23 6WA UK <songs@integrityeurope.com> Used by permission.

MARLBOROUGH GATE   66 66 44 44

1. Beyond all mortal praise
   God's name be ever blest,
   unsearchable his ways,
   his glory manifest;
   from his high throne
   in power and might
   by wisdom's light
   he rules alone.

2. Our times are in his hand
   to whom all flesh is grass,
   while as their Maker planned
   the changing seasons pass.
   He orders all:
   before his eyes
   earth's empires rise,
   her kingdoms fall.

3. He gives to humankind,
   dividing as he will,
   all powers of heart and mind,
   of spirit, strength and skill:
   nor dark nor night
   but must lay bare
   its secrets, where
   he dwells in light.

4. To God the only Lord,
   our fathers' God, be praise;
   his holy name adored
   through everlasting days.
   His mercies trace
   in answered prayer,
   in love and care,
   and gifts of grace.

TIMOTHY DUDLEY-SMITH (b. 1926)
based on Daniel 2.20-23

Music: WAYNE MARSHALL (b. 1961)

SERVANT SONG   87 87

1   Brother, sister, let me serve you,
        let me be as Christ to you;
       pray that I may have the grace
        to let you be my servant too.

2   We are pilgrims on a journey,
        and companions on the road;
       we are here to help each other
        walk the mile and bear the load.

3   I will hold the Christ-light for you
        in the night-time of your fear;
       I will hold my hand out to you,
        speak the peace you long to hear.

4   I will weep when you are weeping;
        when you laugh, I'll laugh with you;
       I will share your joy and sorrow
        till we've seen this journey through.

5   When we sing to God in heaven,
        we shall find such harmony,
       born of all we've known together
        of Christ's love and agony.

6   Brother, sister, let me serve you,
        let me be as Christ to you;
       pray that I may have the grace
        to let you be my servant too.

RICHARD A. M. GILLARD *(b. 1953)*

Music: RICHARD A. M. GILLARD *(b. 1953)*
      arranged by BETTY PULKINGHAM *(b. 1928)*

FINLANDIA   11 10 11 10 extended

1   By gracious powers so wonderfully sheltered
      and confidently waiting, come what may,
      we know that God is with us night and morning,
      and never fails to meet us each new day.

2   Yet are our hearts by their old foe tormented,
      still evil days bring burdens hard to bear;
      O give our frightened souls the sure salvation
      for which, O God, you taught us to prepare.

3   And when the cup you give is filled to brimming
      with bitter suffering, hard to understand,
      we take it gladly, trusting though with trembling,
      out of so good and so beloved a hand.

4   If once again, in this mixed world, you give us
      the joy we had, the brightness of your sun,
      we shall recall what we have learned through sorrow,
      and dedicate our lives to you alone.

DIETRICH BONHOEFFER (1906–1945)
translated by FRED PRATT GREEN (1903–2000)
and KEITH CLEMENTS (*b.* 1943)

The second half of each verse is repeated when this hymn is sung to FINLANDIA.

Music: from the symphonic poem *Finlandia* by
     JEAN SIBELIUS (1865–1957)

264   Words: English versification © Stainer & Bell Ltd for the world, except USA and Canada. Stainer & Bell Ltd, 23 Gruneisen
Road, London N3 1DZ <www.stainer.co.uk>
   264   Words: Adapted by permission of SCM Press from Bonhoeffer's *Powers of Good, Letters and Papers from Prison*, 1971.
    264   Music: © Breitkopf & Härtel, Walkmühlstrasse 52, D-65195 Wiesbaden, Germany. Used by permission.

CLOTH FAIR   86 886

1 Christ be the Lord of all our days,
  the swiftly passing years:
    Lord of our unremembered birth,
    heirs to the brightness of the earth;
  Lord of our griefs and fears.

2 Christ be the source of all our deeds,
  the life our living shares;
    the fount which flows from worlds above
    to never-failing springs of love;
  the ground of all our prayers.

3 Christ be the goal of all our hopes,
  the end to whom we come;
    guide of each pilgrim Christian soul
    which seeks, as compass seeks the pole,
  our many-mansioned home.

4 Christ be the vision of our lives,
  of all we think and are;
    to shine upon our spirits' sight
    as light of everlasting light,
  the bright and morning star.

TIMOTHY DUDLEY-SMITH (b. 1926)

Music: JOHN SCOTT (b. 1956)

EAST STREET 87 83

1   Christ the Way of life possess me,
      lift my heart to love and praise;
      guide and keep, sustain and bless me,
      all my days.

2   Well of life, for ever flowing,
      make my barren soul and bare
      like a watered garden growing,
      fresh and fair.

3   May the Tree of life in splendour
      from its leafy boughs impart
      grace divine and healing tender,
      strength of heart.

4   Path of life before me shining,
      let me come when earth is past,
      sorrow, self and sin resigning,
      home at last.

TIMOTHY DUDLEY-SMITH (b. 1926)

Music: PETER MOGER (b. 1964)

GUITING POWER   85 85 and refrain

1   Christ triumphant, ever reigning,
        Saviour, Master, King!
     Lord of heaven, our lives sustaining,
        hear us as we sing:

        Yours the glory and the crown,
        the high renown, the eternal name.

2   Word incarnate, truth revealing,
        Son of Man on earth!
     power and majesty concealing
        by your humble birth:

3   Suffering servant, scorned, ill-treated,
        victim crucified!
     death is through the cross defeated,
        sinners justified:

4   Priestly king, enthroned for ever
        high in heaven above!
     sin and death and hell shall never
        stifle hymns of love:

Music: JOHN BARNARD (*b.* 1948)

5   So, our hearts and voices raising
through the ages long,
ceaselessly upon you gazing,
this shall be our song:

MICHAEL SAWARD (b. 1932)

BATTLE HYMN OF THE REPUBLIC   77 87 876 and refrain

Refrain

Music: WILLIAM STEFFE *c.* 1852
adapted by NOËL TREDINNICK (*b.* 1949)

1   Come, sing the praise of Jesus,
       sing his love with hearts aflame,
    sing his wondrous birth of Mary
       when to save the world he came;
    tell the life he lived for others
       and his mighty deeds proclaim,
       for Jesus Christ is King.

Praise and glory be to Jesus,
praise and glory be to Jesus,
praise and glory be to Jesus,
for Jesus Christ is King!

2   There's joy for all who serve him,
       more than human tongue can say;
    there is pardon for the sinner,
       and the night is turned to day;
    there is healing for our sorrows,
       there is music all the way,
       for Jesus Christ is King.

3   To Jesus be the glory,
       the dominion and the praise;
    he is Lord of all creation,
       he is guide of all our ways,
    and the world shall be his empire
       in the fullness of the days,
       for Jesus Christ is King.

JACK COPLEY WINSLOW (1882–1974)

ST PAUL'S CATHEDRAL   87 87 D

1   Come with newly written anthems,
        craft your finest psalm or song;
     praise the God of marvellous mercy,
        our deliverer, swift and strong —
     he reveals his holy kindness
        so that all the world may know:
     never once has he forgotten
        what he promised long ago.

2   Bring your hymns of celebration;
        be creative, and rejoice;
     blend as one your skilful playing,
        thankful heart and cheerful voice.
     Let the wonders of God's greatness
        be your focus as you sing;
     weaving reverence and excitement,
        raise the shout: the Lord is King!

3   Sing until the whole creation
        echoes to the melody,
     till the seas and hills and rivers
        join the swelling symphony:
     for he comes, and every nation
        shall receive its just reward —
     sing to greet the God of justice,
        righteous Judge and gracious Lord.

                    MARTIN LECKEBUSCH (b. 1962)
                          based on Psalm 98
Music: PAUL BRYAN (b. 1950)

SAN ROCCO

CM

Alternative lower setting

1 Dear Christ, uplifted from the earth,
   your arms stretched out above
   through every culture, every birth,
   to draw an answering love.

2 Still east and west your love extends
   and always, near and far,
   you call and claim us as your friends
   and love us as we are.

3 Where age and gender, class and race,
   divide us to our shame,
   you see a person and a face,
   a neighbour with a name.

4 May we, accepted as we are,
   yet called in grace to grow,
   reach out to others, near and far
   your healing love to show.

BRIAN WREN (*b.* 1936)

Music: DEREK W. WILLIAMS (1945–2006)

KINGSFOLD   DCM

1   Earth's fragile beauties we possess
       as pilgrim gifts from God,
   and walk the slow and dangerous way
       his wounded feet have trod.
   Though faith by tragedy is rocked,
       and love with pain is scored,
   we sing the pilgrims' song of hope:
       'Your kingdom come, O Lord!'

2   Earth's human longings we possess
       by grief or love compelled
   to take and bear the heavy cross
       Christ's wounded hands have held.
   By cloud and fire he leads us on
       through famine, plague or sword,
   singing with faith the pilgrims' song:
       'Your kingdom come, O Lord!'

3   God's own true image we possess
       in innocence first known,
   now tainted by the hate and spite
       to Christ's own body shown.
   By that same wounded heart of love
       God's image is restored,
   to sing again the pilgrims' song:
       'Your kingdom come, O Lord!'

ROBERT WILLIS (*b.* 1947)

Music: Melody from *English County Songs* 1893
      harmonised by RALPH VAUGHAN WILLIAMS (1872–1958)

HIGHWOOD   11 10 11 10

1   Faith overcomes! The light of Christ is shining,
     piercing the doubt and darkness of our world.
     Walking in trust, we find the way inclining
     to follow in the footsteps of our Lord.

2   Faith overcomes! The truth of God, unfolding
     Wisdom and Word, in cosmic time and space,
     dwells in a single life for our beholding:
     eternal glory in a human face.

3   Faith overcomes! In Jesus God is teaching,
     healing, forgiving, loving to the end;
     to all who know him not his arms outreaching
     from Calv'ry's cross, our Shepherd and our Friend.

4   Faith overcomes! The life of Christ, abundant,
     spent and exhausted in the hour of death,
     bursts from the tomb in mystery triumphant,
     makes us alive through his own Spirit's breath.

5   Faith overcomes! Christ's witnesses have spoken:
     we have not seen, yet now we dare believe
     in him is freedom, peace and joy unbroken,
     a gift to share with all who will receive.

6   Faith overcomes! In Jesus' love abiding,
     we yield ourselves to follow his commands,
     willing to suffer for his name, confiding
     our needs and hopes and fears into his hands.

                              CHRISTOPHER JONES (*b.*1954)

Music: RICHARD RUNCIMAN TERRY (1865–1938)

GOWANBANK   87 87 D

1   For the music of creation,
       for the song your Spirit sings,
   for your sound's divine expression,
       burst of joy in living things:
   God, our God, the world's composer,
       hear us, echoes of your voice:
   music is your art, your glory,
       let the human heart rejoice!

2   Psalms and symphonies exalt you,
       drum and trumpet, string and reed,
   simple melodies acclaim you,
       tunes that rise from deepest need,
   hymns of longing and belonging,
       carols from a cheerful throat,
   lilt of lullaby and love-song
       catching heaven in a note.

3   All the voices of the ages
       in transcendent chorus meet,
   worship lifting up the senses,
       hands that praise and dancing feet;
   over discord and division
       music speaks your joy and peace,
   harmony of earth and heaven,
       song of God that cannot cease!

SHIRLEY ERENA MURRAY (*b.* 1931)

Music: JOHN BARNARD (*b.* 1948)

Give thanks with a grate-ful heart,— give thanks to the Ho-ly One,— give thanks____ be-cause he's gi-ven____ Je-sus Christ,_____ his Son.

1st & 3rd times Give Son.

2nd & 4th times And now let the weak say, 'I am strong!' Let the poor say, 'I am rich be-cause of what the Lord has done for____ us!' And now let the weak say, 'I am strong!' Let the poor say, 'I am rich be-cause of what the Lord has done for____ *Final time to Coda*

D.S. al Coda us!' Give us!'

✢ *Coda* Give thanks.

HENRY SMITH (*b.*1952)

Music: HENRY SMITH (*b.*1952)

ST HELEN 87 87 447

1 God beyond earth's finest treasures,
   you alone shall have my praise;
I will love your cherished people,
   I will serve you all my days;
      be my ruler,
      be my refuge,
   God the guardian of my ways.

2 You have caused my life to prosper —
   countless gifts your love has planned!
Day and night your wisdom prompts me,
   shows me all that you command;
      God before me,
      God beside me,
   safe within your care I stand.

3 When my earthly days are over,
   fresh delights remain in store:
vaster riches, fuller pleasures
   than I ever knew before —
      life unending,
      joy unfading
   in your presence evermore.

MARTIN LECKEBUSCH (b. 1962)
based on Psalm 16

Music: GEORGE CLEMENT MARTIN (1844–1916)

FAITHFULNESS   11 10 11 10 and refrain

Refrain

Great is thy faith - ful - ness! Great is thy faith - ful - ness!

Morn - ing by morn - ing new mer - cies I see;

all I have need - ed thy hand has pro - vi - ded,

great is thy faith - ful - ness, Lord, un - to me.

1   Great is thy faithfulness, O God my Father,
      there is no shadow of turning with thee;
      thou changest not, thy compassions they fail not,
      as thou hast been thou for ever wilt be.

2   Summer and winter, and spring-time and harvest,
      sun, moon and stars in their courses above,
      join with all nature in manifold witness
      to thy great faithfulness, mercy and love.

3   Pardon for sin and a peace that endureth,
      thine own dear presence to cheer and to guide;
      strength for today and bright hope for tomorrow,
      blessings all mine, with ten thousand beside!

THOMAS O. CHISHOLM (1866–1960)

Music: WILLIAM W. MARION RUNYAN (1870–1957)

1 Ho—ly, ho—ly, ho—ly is the Lord; ho—ly is the Lord God al—migh—ty. Ho—ly, ho—ly, ho—ly is the Lord; ho—ly is the Lord God al—migh—ty, who was, and is and is to come. Ho—ly, ho—ly, ho—ly is the Lord!

Music: Melody source unknown
arranged by ANNE HARRISON (b. 1954) and others

1   Holy, holy, holy is the Lord;
     holy is the Lord God almighty.
     Holy, holy, holy is the Lord;
     holy is the Lord God almighty,
        who was, and is, and is to come.
     Holy, holy, holy is the Lord!

2   Jesus, Jesus, Jesus is the Lord;
     Jesus is the Lord God almighty.
     Jesus, Jesus, Jesus is the Lord;
     Jesus is the Lord God almighty,
        who was, and is, and is to come.
     Jesus, Jesus, Jesus is the Lord!

3   Worthy, worthy, worthy is the Lord;
     worthy is the Lord God almighty.
     Worthy, worthy, worthy is the Lord;
     worthy is the Lord God almighty,
        who was, and is, and is to come!
     Worthy, worthy, worthy is the Lord.

4   Glory, glory, glory to the Lord;
     glory to the Lord God almighty.
     Glory, glory, glory to the Lord;
     glory to the Lord God almighty,
        who was, and is, and is to come.
     Glory, glory, glory to the Lord.

                                    Anonymous

*Verses 1, 2 and 4 may be sung at various points during
the Eucharistic Prayer at Holy Communion.*

Holy is God, holy and strong!
God ever living, alleluia!

1   Sing the Lord's praise, every nation,
    give him all honour and glory.
    Strong is his love for his people,
    his faithfulness is eternal.

2   Praise to the Father almighty;
    praise to his Son, Christ the Lord;
    praise to the life-giving Spirit,
    both now and forever. Amen.

PAUL INWOOD (b. 1947)
based on Psalm 117

Music: PAUL INWOOD (b. 1947)

1 How long, O Lord, will you for-get an an-swer to my prayer?___ No to-kens of your love I see, your face is turned a-way from me; I wres-tle with des-pair.

2   How long, O Lord, will you forsake
     and leave me in this way?
     When will you come to my relief?
     My heart is overwhelmed with grief,
     by evil night and day.

3   How long, O Lord — but you forgive,
     with mercy from above.
     I find that all your ways are just,
     I learn to praise you and to trust
     in your unfailing love.

BARBARA WOOLLETT (*b.* 1937)
based on Psalm 13

Music: CHRISTOPHER NORTON (*b.* 1953)

280

COE FEN   DCM

1   How shall I sing that majesty
      which angels do admire?
  Let dust in dust and silence lie;
      sing, sing, ye heavenly choir.
  Thousands of thousands stand around
      thy throne, O God most high;
  ten thousand times ten thousand sound
      thy praise; but who am I?

2   Thy brightness unto them appears,
      while I thy footsteps trace;
  a sound of God comes to my ears,
      but they behold thy face:
  I shall, I fear, be dark and cold,
      with all my fire and light;
  yet when thou dost accept their gold,
      Lord, treasure up my mite.

3   Enlighten with faith's light my heart,
      inflame it with love's fire,
  then shall I sing and bear a part
      with that celestial choir.
  They sing, because thou art their sun;
      Lord, send a beam on me;
  for where heaven is but once begun,
      there alleluias be.

4   How great a being, Lord, is thine,
      which doth all beings keep!
  Thy knowledge is the only line
      to sound so vast a deep:
  thou art a sea without a shore,
      a sun without a sphere;
  thy time is now and evermore,
      thy place is everywhere.

* JOHN MASON (*c.*1645–1694)

Music: KENNETH NAYLOR (1931–1991)

279   Words: © Barbara Woollett / Jubilate Hymns. Administered by The Jubilate Group, 4 Thorne Park Road, Torquay TQ2
      6RX <copyrightmanager@jubilate.co.uk> Used by permission.
279   Music: © 1991 HarperCollinsReligious. Administered by Song Solutions CopyCare, 14 Horsted Square, Uckfield, East
      Sussex, TN22 1QG, United Kingdom. <info@songsolutions.org> Used by permission.

RICHMOND   CM

1   I am the Light whose brightness shines
        on every pilgrim's way,
    and brings to evil's darkest place
        the glorious light of day.

2   I am the Gate that leads to life
        along the narrow way,
    the Shepherd who will tend my sheep
        that none are lost or stray.

3   I am the Well from whose fresh springs
        life-giving water flows
    and on each side the tree of life
        with leaves for healing grows.

4   I am the Bread, God's gift from heaven,
        sent down to satisfy
    that hunger which cries out for food;
        who eats shall never die.

5   I am the Vine whose branches grow
        united in one root;
    who dwell in me, and I in them,
        shall live and bear much fruit.

6   I am the Resurrection life,
        the power of God whereby
    whoever truly trusts in me
        shall live and never die.

7   I am the Way, the Truth, the Life,
        and truth shall set you free
    to seek and find the way to life
        and live that life in me.

ROBERT WILLIS (b. 1947)

Music: Melody by THOMAS HAWEIS (1734–1820)
    harmonised by SAMUEL WEBBE , *the younger* (c. 1770–1843)

1 I do not know tomorrow's way,
     if dark or bright its hours may be;
   but I know Christ, and come what may,
     I know that he abides with me.

2 I do not know what may befall
     of grief or gladness, peace or pain;
   but I know Christ, and through it all
     I know his presence will sustain.

3 I do not know when evening falls,
     if soon or late earth's day grows dim;
   but I know Christ, and when he calls,
     I know he'll call me home to him.

MARGARET CLARKSON (1915–2008)

Music: JILL SUTHERAN
    arranged by ANNE HARRISON (b.1954) and TIM RUFFER (b.1960)

HYFRYDOL

87 87 D

Music: ROWLAND HUW PRICHARD (1811–1887)
harmonised by Compilers of *English Hymnal,* 1906

1   I will sing the wondrous story
of the Christ who died for me,
how he left the realms of glory
for the cross on Calvary.
Yes, I'll sing the wondrous story
of the Christ who died for me —
sing it with his saints in glory,
gathered by the crystal sea.

2   I was lost but Jesus found me,
found the sheep that went astray,
raised me up and gently led me
back into the narrow way.
Days of darkness still may meet me,
sorrow's path I oft may tread;
but his presence still is with me,
by his guiding hand I'm led.

3   He will keep me till the river
rolls its waters at my feet:
then he'll bear me safely over,
made by grace for glory meet.
Yes, I'll sing the wondrous story
of the Christ who died for me —
sing it with his saints in glory,
gathered by the crystal sea.

FRANCIS HAROLD ROWLEY (1854–1952)

Music: DAVE RUIS

Refrain

I will give— you all my— wor - ship, I will give— you

ways.———— I will give— you all my— wor - ship, I will give— you
you— a-lone.—

all my praise.———— You a-lone— I long to—— wor - ship,

you a-lone— are wor - thy of— my——— praise.—

1   I will worship (I will worship)
with all of my heart (with all of my heart).
I will praise you (I will praise you)
with all of my strength (all my strength).
I will seek you (I will seek you)
all of my days (all of my days).
I will follow (I will follow)
all of your ways (all your ways).

> *I will give you all my worship,*
> *I will give you all my praise.*
> *You alone I long to worship,*
> *you alone are worthy of my praise.*

2   I will bow down (I will bow down),
hail you as King (hail you as King).
I will serve you (I will serve you),
give you everything (give you everything).
I will lift up (I will lift up)
my eyes to your throne (my eyes to your throne).
I will trust you (I will trust you),
I will trust you alone (trust in you alone).

DAVE RUIS

GREAT CHEVERELL   10 10 and refrain

1 I'll praise the Lord for ever and ever, my
soul shall boast of his wonderful name: *Glorify the
Lord with me; exalt his name, for great is he! I'll
praise the Lord for ever and ever.*

2   I sought the Lord, he answered my calling,
     delivered me from my innermost fears:

3   O taste and see how gracious the Lord is:
     secure are they who take refuge in him:

4   The Lord redeems the faithful who serve him,
     and those who trust him he never condemns:

PAUL WIGMORE (b.1925)
based on Psalm 34.1-8,22

Music: JOHN BARNARD (b.1948)

286

1 In Christ alone my hope is found, he is my light, my strength, my
song; this Cornerstone, this solid Ground, firm through the
fiercest drought and storm. What heights of love, what depths of

peace, when fears are stilled, when stri-vings cease! My Com-for-

-ter, my All in All, here in the love of Christ I

stand.

2   In Christ alone! — who took on flesh,
fullness of God in helpless babe!
This gift of love and righteousness,
scorned by the ones he came to save:
till on that cross as Jesus died,
the wrath of God was satisfied —
for every sin on him was laid;
here in the death of Christ I live.

3   There in the ground his body lay,
light of the world by darkness slain:
Then bursting forth in glorious day
up from the grave he rose again!
And as he stands in victory
sin's curse has lost its grip on me,
for I am his and he is mine —
bought with the precious blood of Christ.

4   No guilt in life, no fear in death,
this is the power of Christ in me;
from life's first cry to final breath,
Jesus commands my destiny.
No power of hell, no scheme of man,
can ever pluck me from his hand;
till he returns or calls me home,
here in the power of Christ I'll stand!

STUART TOWNEND (b. 1963)
and KEITH GETTY (b. 1974)

Music: STUART TOWNEND (b. 1963) and KEITH GETTY (b. 1974)

ENGELBERG   10 10 10 and Alleluia

1   Let us rejoice: God's gift to us is peace!
    Here is the calm which bids our strivings cease,
    for God's acceptance brings a true release:
    alleluia!

2   We can be strong, for now we stand by grace,
    held in his loving, fatherly embrace;
    his care remains, whatever trials we face:
    alleluia!

3   We trust in God, and shall not be dismayed,
    nor find our hopes of glory are betrayed,
    for all his splendour we shall see displayed:
    alleluia!

4   And come what may, we never need despair —
    God is at work through all the griefs we bear,
    that in the end his likeness we may share:
    alleluia!

5   Deep in our hearts the love of God is found;
    his precious gifts of life and joy abound —
    so let our finest songs of praise resound:
    alleluia!

MARTIN LECKEBUSCH (*b.* 1962)
based on Romans 5.1-5

Music: CHARLES VILLIERS STANFORD (1852–1924)
arranged by Compilers of *BBC Hymn Book*, 1951

OLD YEAVERING 888 7

QUEM PASTORES LAUDAVERE 888 7

1 Like a mighty river flowing,
   like a flower in beauty growing,
   far beyond all human knowing
      is the perfect peace of God.

2 Like the hills serene and even,
   like the coursing clouds of heaven,
   like the heart that's been forgiven
      is the perfect peace of God.

3 Like the summer breezes playing,
   like the tall trees softly swaying,
   like the lips of silent praying
      is the perfect peace of God.

4 Like the morning sun ascended,
   like the scents of evening blended,
   like a friendship never ended
      is the perfect peace of God.

5 Like the azure ocean swelling,
   like the jewel all-excelling,
   far beyond our human telling
      is the perfect peace of God.

MICHAEL PERRY (1942–1996)

Music: 1: NOËL TREDINNICK (*b.* 1949)
Music: 2: German 15th-century melody
   adapted by RALPH VAUGHAN WILLIAMS (1872–1958)

LORD OF THE YEARS

11 10 11 10

Descant (v. 5)

5 Lord,___ in liv-ing power re-make___ us,

Unison

5 Lord, for our-selves; in liv-ing power re-make us,

self on the cross___ and___ Christ up-on the throne;

self on the cross and Christ up-on___ the throne;

for___ the fu - - ture take___ us,

past put be-hind us, for the fu - ture take us,

Lord of our lives,___ to___ live for Christ a - lone.

Lord of our lives. to live for Christ a - lone.

1 Lord, for the years your love has kept and guided,
urged and inspired us, cheered us on our way,
sought us and saved us, pardoned and provided,
Lord of the years, we bring our thanks today.

2 Lord, for that word, the word of life which fires us,
speaks to our hearts and sets our souls ablaze,
teaches and trains, rebukes us and inspires us,
Lord of the word, receive your people's praise.

3 Lord, for our land, in this our generation,
spirits oppressed by pleasure, wealth and care;
for young and old, for commonwealth and nation,
Lord of our land, be pleased to hear our prayer.

4 Lord, for our world; when we disown and doubt him,
loveless in strength, and comfortless in pain;
hungry and helpless, lost indeed without him,
Lord of the world, we pray that Christ may reign.

5 Lord, for ourselves; in living power remake us,
self on the cross and Christ upon the throne;
past put behind us, for the future take us,
Lord of our lives, to live for Christ alone.

TIMOTHY DUDLEY-SMITH (b. 1926)

Music: MICHAEL BAUGHEN (b. 1930)
arranged by DAVID ILIFF (b. 1939)
alternative harmony and descant by JOHN BARNARD (b. 1948)

O WALY WALY   LM

1.   Lord, make us servants of your peace:
     where there is hate, may we sow love;
   where there is hurt, may we forgive;
     where there is strife, may we make one.

2.   Where all is doubt, may we sow faith;
     where all is gloom, may we sow hope;
   where all is night, may we sow light;
     where all is tears, may we sow joy.

3.   Jesus, our Lord, may we not seek
     to be consoled, but to console,
   nor look to understanding hearts,
     but look for hearts to understand.

4.   May we not look for love's return,
     but seek to love unselfishly,
   for in our giving we receive,
     and in forgiving are forgiven.

5.   Dying we live, and are reborn
     through death's dark night to endless day;
   Lord, make us servants of your peace
     to wake at last in heaven's light.

JAMES QUINN, SJ   (1919–2010)
after FRANCIS OF ASSISI   (1182–1226)

Music: English traditional melody
    arranged by NOËL TREDINNICK (b. 1949)

FAIRMEAD   9 10 11 10

1   Lord, you are the light of life to me;
     when darkness hides my path, you help me see.
     Shine on me, O Lord, that now and all my days
     your light may lead me on, guiding my ways.

2   Lord, you are the rock on which I stand,
     stable and strong in you, held by your hand.
     Keep me safe, O Lord; in weakness let there be
     your loving, firm embrace upholding me.

3   Lord, you are the truth that sets me free;
     only in you is found true liberty.
     Teach me then, O Lord, in all things to pursue
     your good and perfect will, growing like you.

4   Lord, you are the Lamb of God who died,
     suff'ring for love of me, scorned, crucified.
     Love me still, O Lord; let others daily see
     your selfless, serving love flowing through me.

5   Lord, you are the King who ever reigns.
     Earth's rulers rise and fall: your throne remains.
     Rule my life, O Lord; I yield myself anew
     your name to glorify, living for you.

BRIAN HOARE (b. 1935)

Music: BRIAN HOARE (b. 1935)

GREAT STANMORE   IO IO IO IO

Unison

1   Love is the touch of intangible joy;
     love is the force that no fear can destroy;
     love is the goodness we gladly applaud:
        God is where love is, for love is of God.

2   Love is the lilt in a lingering voice;
     love is the hope that can make us rejoice;
     love is the cure for the frightened and flawed:
        God is where love is, for love is of God.

3   Love is the light in the tunnel of pain;
     love is the will to be whole once again;
     love is the trust of a friend on the road:
        God is where love is, for love is of God.

4   Love is the Maker and Spirit and Son:
     love is the kingdom their will has begun;
     love is the path which the saints all have trod:
        God is where love is, for love is of God.

ALISON ROBERTSON (*b.* 1940)

Music: JOHN BARNARD (*b.* 1948)

CALON LÂN 77 77 D

1   Loved with everlasting love,
     led by grace that love to know;
  Spirit, breathing from above,
     you have taught me it is so.
  O what full and perfect peace,
     joy and wonder all divine!
  In a love which cannot cease
     I am his, and he is mine.

2   Heaven above is softer blue,
     earth around is richer green;
  something lives in every hue,
     Christless eyes have never seen:
  songs of birds in sweetness grow,
     flowers with deeper beauties shine,
  since I know, as now I know,
     I am his and he is mine.

3   His for ever, his alone!
     Who the Lord from me shall part?
  With what joy and peace unknown
     Christ can fill the loving heart!
  Heaven and earth may pass away,
     sun and stars in gloom decline,
  but of Christ I still shall say:
     I am his and he is mine.

* GEORGE WADE ROBINSON (1838–1877)

Music: JOHN HUGHES (1872–1914)
    arranged by JOHN BARNARD (b. 1948)

1 Meek-ness and ma-jes-ty, man-hood and de-i-ty, in per-fect
har-mo-ny — the Man who is God: Lord of e-ter-ni-ty
dwells in hu-man-i-ty, kneels in hu-mil-i-ty__ and__ wash-es our
feet.

Refrain

Oh, what a mys-te-ry, meek-ness and ma-jes-ty.___

Bow down and wor-ship,___ for

this is your God,___ this is your

vv. 1,2   *v. 3*

God!___

Music: GRAHAM KENDRICK (*b.* 1950)
   arranged by CHRISTOPHER NORTON (*b.* 1953)

1   Meekness and majesty,
    manhood and deity,
    in perfect harmony,
        the Man who is God.
    Lord of eternity
    dwells in humanity,
    kneels in humility
        and washes our feet.

        Oh, what a mystery,
        meekness and majesty.
        Bow down and worship
        for this is your God,
        this is your God.

2   Father's pure radiance,
    perfect in innocence,
    yet learns obedience
        to death on a cross.
    Suffering to give us life,
    conquering through sacrifice,
    and as they crucify
        prays: 'Father, forgive.'

3   Wisdom unsearchable,
    God the invisible,
    Love indestructible
        in frailty appears.
    Lord of infinity,
    stooping so tenderly,
    lifts our humanity
        to the heights of his throne.

                GRAHAM KENDRICK   (b. 1950)

My Je - sus, my Sav - iour, Lord, there is none_ like_ you..

_ All of my days__ I want to praise _ the won-ders of your

migh - ty love. My com - fort, my shel - ter,

tow-er of re - fuge and strength, let ev-ery breath,_ all that I am,_

_ nev - er cease to wor - - ship you.

Shout to the Lord_ all the earth,_ let us sing,_____ pow-er and ma -
I sing for joy__ at the work__ of your hands.___ For - ev - er I'll love

- - jes - ty, praise__ to the King.__ Mountains bow down_ and the seas_
_ you, for - ev - - er I'll stand._ No-thing com-pares_ to the pro -

1st time

_ will roar__ at the sound____ of your name.____

2nd time

- - mise I have__ in you._____

Music: DARLENE ZSCHECH (*b.* 1965)

My Jesus, my Saviour,
Lord, there is none like you.
All of my days I want to praise
the wonders of your mighty love.
My comfort, my shelter,
tower of refuge and strength,
let every breath, all that I am,
never cease to worship you.

Shout to the Lord all the earth, let us sing
power and majesty, praise to the King.
Mountains bow down
and the seas will roar at the sound of your name.
I sing for joy at the work of your hands.
Forever I'll love you, forever I'll stand.
Nothing compares to the promise I have in you.

DARLENE ZSCHECH (b. 1965)

295 Words and Music: © 1993, Darlene Zschech / Hillsong Publishing / kingswaysongs.com. Thankyou Music. Administered (UK and Europe) by kingswaysongs.com <tym@kingsway.co.uk>. Remaining territories administered by worshiptogether.com songs. Used by permission.

HOW CAN I KEEP FROM   87 87 and refrain

1 My life flows on in endless song above earth's la - men - ta - tion: _ I catch the sweet, though far - off hymn that hails a new cre - a - tion. _

Refrain, Harmony

No storm can shake my in - most calm while to that Rock I'm cling - ing; _ since love is Lord of ___ heaven and earth, how can I keep from sing - ing? _

Music: American traditional melody
     arranged by Compilers of *Common Ground*, 1998

1   My life flows on in endless song
       above earth's lamentation:
     I catch the sweet, though far-off hymn
       that sings a new creation.

       No storm can shake my inmost calm
         while to that Rock I'm clinging;
       since love is Lord of heaven and earth,
         how can I keep from singing?

2   Through all the tumult and the strife
       I hear that music ringing;
     it finds an echo in my soul;
       how can I keep from singing?

3   What though my joys and comforts die?
       The Lord my Saviour liveth!
     What though the darkness round me close?
       Songs in the night he giveth.

4   The peace of Christ makes fresh my heart,
       a fountain ever springing.
     All things are mine since I am his!
       How can I keep from singing?

ROBERT LOWRY (1826–1899) and DORIS PLENN
after an early Quaker song

1 My soul finds rest in God a-lone, my rock and my sal-va-tion; a fort-ress strong a-gainst my foes, and I will not be sha-ken. Though lips may bless and hearts may curse, and lies like ar-rows pierce me, I'll fix my heart on righteousness, I'll look to him who hears me. O praise him, hal-le-lu-jah, my de-light and my re-ward; ev-er-last-ing, nev-er fail-ing, my Re-deem-er, my God.

Refrain

vv. 1,2   *v. 3*

2 My

Music: AARON KEYES and STUART TOWNEND (*b.* 1963)

1 My soul finds rest in God alone,
    my rock and my salvation;
  a fortress strong against my foes,
    and I will not be shaken.
  Though lips may bless and hearts may curse,
    and lies like arrows pierce me,
  I'll fix my heart on righteousness,
    I'll look to him who hears me.

O praise him, hallelujah, my delight and my reward;
everlasting, never failing, my Redeemer, my God.

2 My soul finds rest in God alone
    amid the world's temptations;
  when evil seeks to take a hold
    I'll cling to my salvation.
  Though riches come and riches go,
    don't set your heart upon them;
  the fields of hope in which I sow
    are harvested in heaven.

3 I'll set my gaze on God alone
    and trust in him completely;
  with every day pour out my soul
    and he will prove his mercy.
  Though life is but a fleeting breath,
    a sigh too brief to measure,
  my King has crushed the curse of death
    and I am his for ever.

AARON KEYES
and STUART TOWNEND (b. 1963)
based on Psalm 62

297 Words and Music: © 2007, Thankyou Music. Administered (UK and Europe) by kingswaysongs.com
<tym@kingsway.co.uk>. Remaining territories administered by worshiptogether.com songs. Used by permission.

WILTSHIRE   CM

1   O changeless Christ, for ever new,
        who walked our earthly ways,
        still draw our hearts as once you drew
        the hearts of other days.

2   As once you spoke by plain and hill
        or taught by shore and sea,
        so be today our teacher still,
        O Christ of Galilee.

3   As wind and storm their Master heard
        and his command fulfilled,
        may troubled hearts receive your word,
        the tempest-tossed be stilled.

4   And as of old to all who prayed
        your healing hand was shown,
        so be your touch upon us laid,
        unseen but not unknown.

5   In broken bread, in wine outpoured,
        your new and living way
        proclaim to us, O risen Lord,
        O Christ of this our day.

6   O changeless Christ, till life is past
        your blessing still be given;
        then bring us home, to taste at last
        the timeless joys of heaven.

TIMOTHY DUDLEY-SMITH (b. 1926)

Music: GEORGE THOMAS SMART (1776–1867)

THAXTED   76 76 T

Unison

1 O God beyond all praising,
     we worship you today
   and sing the love amazing
     that songs cannot repay;
   for we can only wonder
     at every gift you send,
   at blessings without number
     and mercies without end:
   we lift our hearts before you
     and wait upon your word,
   we honour and adore you,
     our great and mighty Lord.

2 Then hear, O gracious Saviour,
     accept the love we bring,
   that we who know your favour
     may serve you as our king;
   and whether our tomorrows
     be filled with good or ill,
   we'll triumph through our sorrows
     and rise to bless you still:
   to marvel at your beauty
     and glory in your ways,
   and make a joyful duty
     our sacrifice of praise.

MICHAEL PERRY (1942–1996)

Music: from *The Planets,* by
    GUSTAV HOLST (1874–1934)
    adapted by Compilers of *Hymns Ancient & Modern Revised,* 1950

SOLI DEO GLORIA

99 999 and refrain

Steadily

1 O God of blessings, all praise to you! Your love sur-rounds us our_

whole life through. You are the free-dom of those op-pressed; you are the

com-fort of all dis-tressed. Come now, O ho-ly and wel-come

Refrain

guest: So - li____ De - o glo - ri - a!

vv. 1 - 5 *rit.* *v. 6*

So - li____ De - o glo - ri - a! - a!

Music: MARTY HAUGEN (*b.* 1950)

1   O God of blessings, all praise to you!
Your love surrounds us our whole life through.
You are the freedom of those oppressed;
you are the comfort of all distressed.
Come now, O holy and welcome guest:
   Soli Deo gloria! Soli Deo gloria!

2   All praise for wisdom, great gift sublime,
through words and teachers of every time;
for stories ancient and knowledge new,
for coaches, mentors, and counsellors true
whose life of service brought us to you:

3   All praise for prophets, through grace inspired
to preach and witness with hearts on fire.
Your Spirit chooses the weak and small
to sing the new reign where mighty fall;
with them may we live your gospel call:

4   All praise for music, deep gift profound,
through hands and voices in holy sound;
the psalms of David, and Mary's praise,
in wordless splendour and lyric phrase,
with all creation one song we raise:

5   All praise for Jesus, best gift divine
through word and witness, in bread and wine;
incarnate love song of boundless grace,
priest, teacher, prophet in time and space,
your steadfast kindness with human face:

6   A billion voices in one great song,
now soft and gentle, now deep and strong,
in every culture and style and key,
from hill and valley, with sky and sea,
with Christ we praise you eternally:

MARTY HAUGEN (*b.* 1950)

'Soli Deo gloria!' — *'To God alone be glory!'*

1.   O God, you search me and you know me.
        All my thoughts lie open to your gaze.
     When I walk or lie down you are before me:
        ever the maker and keeper of my days.

2.   You know my resting and my rising.
        You discern my purpose from afar,
     and with love everlasting you besiege me:
        in every moment of life and death, you are.

3.   Before a word is on my tongue, Lord,
        you have known its meaning through and through.
     You are with me beyond my understanding:
        God of my present, my past and future, too.

4.   Although your Spirit is upon me,
        still I search for shelter from your light.
     There is nowhere on earth I can escape you:
        even the darkness is radiant in your sight.

5.   For you created me and shaped me,
        gave me life within my mother's womb.
     For the wonder of who I am, I praise you:
        safe in your hands, all creation is made new.

BERNADETTE FARRELL (*b.* 1957)
based on Psalm 139

Music: BERNADETTE FARRELL (*b.* 1957)

1 Oh, the mer-cy of God, the glo-ry of grace, that you chose to re-deem us, to for-give and re-store; and you call us your child-ren, cho-sen in him to be ho-ly and blame-less to the glo-ry of God.

2 Oh, the rich-ness of grace, the depths of his love, in him is re-demp-tion, the for-give-ness of sin; you called us as right-eous, pre-des-tined in him for the praise of his glo-ry, in-clu-ded in Christ.

3 Oh, the glo-ry of God ex-pressed in his Son, his i-mage and like-ness re-vealed to us all; the plea of the a-ges com-ple-ted in Christ: that we be pre-sen-ted per-fect-ed in him.

Refrain

To the praise of his glo-ri-ous grace, to the praise of his glo-ry and power; to him be all glo-ry, ho-nour and praise for ev-er and ev-er and ev-er, a-men.

GEOFF BULLOCK (b. 1956)

Music: GEOFF BULLOCK (b. 1956)

VICARS' CLOSE   76 76 D

3 Now by prince_____ and peo - ple let his praise be told;
praise him, men and mai - - dens, praise him, young and old.
He, the Lord of glo - - ry! We his praise pro - claim!
High a - bove all hea - vens mag - ni - fy his name!

Music: MALCOLM ARCHER (*b.* 1952)

1   Praise the Lord of heaven,
    praise him in the height;
    praise him, all his angels,
    praise him, hosts of light.
    Sun and moon together,
    shining stars aflame,
    planets in their courses,
    magnify his name!

2   Earth and ocean praise him;
    mountains, hills and trees;
    fire and hail and tempest,
    wind and storm and seas.
    Praise him, fields and forests,
    birds on flashing wings,
    praise him, beasts and cattle,
    all created things.

3   Now by prince and people
    let his praise be told;
    praise him, men and maidens,
    praise him, young and old.
    He, the Lord of glory!
    We his praise proclaim!
    High above all heavens
    magnify his name!

TIMOTHY DUDLEY-SMITH (b. 1926)
based on Psalm 148

NETTLETON   87 87 D

1   Praise the One who breaks the darkness
       with a liberating light.
    Praise the One who frees the prisoners
       turning blindness into sight.
    Praise the One who preached the gospel,
       curing every dread disease,
    calming storms and feeding thousands
       with the very bread of peace.

2   Praise the One who blessed the children
       with a strong yet gentle word.
    Praise the One who drove out demons
       with a piercing, two-edged sword.
    Praise the One who brings cool water
       to the desert's burning sand;
    from this well comes living water,
       quenching thirst in every land.

3   Praise the one true love incarnate,
       Christ, who suffered in our place.
    Jesus died and rose for many
       that we may know God by grace.
    Let us sing for joy and gladness,
       seeing what our God has done.
    Praise the one redeeming glory.
       Praise the One who makes us one.

RUSTY EDWARDS *(b. 1955)*

Music: American melody in Wyeth's *Repository of Sacred Music, Part II,* 1813
arranged by JOHN WILSON (1905–1992)

YANWORTH   10 10 10 10

Unison

1   Ring out the bells, and let the people know
     that God is worshipped by the church below:
       to all around this truth the bells declare —
       'Your needs are lifted up to God in prayer!'

2   Ring out the bells, and let the people hear —
     let hearts be open now, and faith draw near;
       receive the grace that only God can give —
       by word and symbol feed and grow and live.

3   Ring out the bells, and let the people sing
     through changing seasons to our changeless King:
       all perfect gifts are sent us from above —
       respond with praises for such faithful love.

4   Ring out the bells until that glorious day
     when death shall die and sin be done away:
       then comes our God so everyone shall see —
       let all the bells ring out in victory!

MICHAEL PERRY (1942–1996)

Music: JOHN BARNARD (b. 1948)

BUNILLIDH 98 98

1 Safe in the hands of God who made me,
    what can there be that I should fear?
    God is my light and my salvation,
      strong is his help when foes are near.

2 This I have prayed and will seek after,
    that I may walk with God each day;
    then will he give me his protection,
      no trouble shall my heart dismay.

3 God of my life, my Lord, my master,
    father and mother now to me:
    come, shield me from the threat of evil,
      open your hands and set me free!

4 Teach me your way and lead me onwards,
    save me from those who do me wrong;
    give me the grace to wait with patience,
      help me to trust, hold firm, be strong.

MICHAEL PERRY (1942–1996)
based on Psalm 27

Music: Melody by DONALD MACDONALD (*b.* 1944)
    harmonised by ISOBEL GORDON (*b.* 1969)

CROSS OF JESUS   87 87

1 Sing, my soul, when hope is sleeping,
  sing when faith gives way to fears;
 sing to melt the ice of sadness,
  making way for joy through tears.

2 Sing, my soul, when sickness lingers,
  sing to dull the sharpest pain;
 sing to set the spirit leaping:
  healing needs a glad refrain.

3 Sing, my soul, of him who shaped me,
  let me wander far away,
 ran with open arms to greet me,
  brought me home again to stay.

4 Sing, my soul, when light seems darkest,
  sing when night refuses rest,
 sing though death should mock the future:
  what's to come by God is blessed.

JOHN L. BELL (*b.*1949)
and GRAHAM MAULE (*b.*1958)

Music: JOHN STAINER (1840–1901)
 from *The Crucifixion*, 1887

307 Words: From *Enemy of Apathy*, 1988. © 1988, Wild Goose Resource Group, The Iona Community, 4th Floor, Savoy
Centre, 140 Sauchiehall Street, Glasgow G2 3DH

CREATOR GOD   86 446

Music: NORMAN WARREN (*b.* 1934)
     harmonised by Compilers of *Common Ground,* 1998

1   Safe in the shadow of the Lord
    beneath his hand and power,
      I trust in him,
      I trust in him,
    my fortress and my tower.

2   My hope is set on God alone
    though Satan spreads his snare;
      I trust in him,
      I trust in him,
    to keep me in his care.

3   From fears and phantoms of the night,
    from foes about my way,
      I trust in him,
      I trust in him,
    by darkness as by day.

4   His holy angels keep my feet
    secure from every stone;
      I trust in him,
      I trust in him,
    and unafraid go on.

5   Strong in the everlasting Name,
    and in my Father's care,
      I trust in him,
      I trust in him,
    who hears and answers prayer.

6   Safe in the shadow of the Lord,
    possessed by love divine,
      I trust in him,
      I trust in him,
    and meet his love with mine.

TIMOTHY DUDLEY-SMITH (b. 1926)
based on Psalm 91

SING OF THE LORD'S GOODNESS   12 7 12 7 and refrain

Music: ERNEST SANDS (*b.* 1949) and CHRISTOPHER WALKER (*b.* 1947)
       arranged by PAUL INWOOD (*b.* 1947)

1   Sing of the Lord's goodness, Father of all wisdom,
       come to him and bless his name.
    Mercy he has shown us, his love is for ever,
       faithful to the end of days.

> *Come then, all you nations, sing of your Lord's goodness,*
>   *melodies of praise and thanks to God.*
> *Ring out the Lord's glory, praise him with your music,*
>   *worship him and bless his name.*

2   Power he has wielded, honour is his garment,
       risen from the snares of death.
    His word he has spoken, one bread he has broken,
       new life he now gives to all.

3   Courage in our darkness, comfort in our sorrow,
       Spirit of our God most high;
    solace for the weary, pardon for the sinner,
       splendour of the living God.

4   Praise him with your singing, praise him with the trumpet,
       praise God with the lute and harp;
    praise him with the cymbals, praise him with your dancing,
       praise God till the end of days.

ERNEST SANDS (b. 1949)

309 Words and Music: © 1981 Ernest Sands. Published by OCP Publications,
5536 NE Hassalo, Portland, OR 97213, USA. All rights reserved. Used with permission.

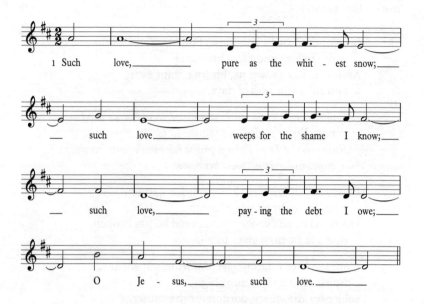

1 Such love, _____ pure as the whit - est snow; _____
_ such love _____ weeps for the shame I know; _____
_ such love, _____ pay - ing the debt I owe; _____
O Je - sus, _____ such love. _____

2   Such love, stilling my restlessness;
     such love, filling my emptiness;
     such love, showing me holiness;
         O Jesus, such love.

3   Such love, springs from eternity;
     such love, streaming through history;
     such love, fountain of life to me;
         O Jesus, such love.

GRAHAM KENDRICK (b. 1950)

Music: GRAHAM KENDRICK (b. 1950)
     arranged by CHRISTOPHER NORTON (b. 1953)

TAKE THIS MOMENT   75 75

1 Take this mo - ment, sign,__ and__
space; take my friends a - - round;_____
here a - mong__ us____ make__ the____ place
where your love is found._____

2   Take the time to call my name,
     take the time to mend
   who I am and what I've been,
    all I've failed to tend.

3   Take the tiredness of my days,
     take my past regret,
   letting your forgiveness touch
    all I can't forget.

4   Take the little child in me
     scared of growing old;
   help me here to find my worth
    made in Christ's own mould.

5   Take my talents, take my skills,
     take what's yet to be;
   let my life be yours, and yet
    let it still be me.

JOHN L. BELL (b. 1949)
and GRAHAM MAULE (b. 1958)

Music: JOHN L. BELL (b. 1949)

STAND UP   76 76 D
Unison

1   The heavens proclaim God's glory,
        the skies sing out in praise,
     extolling their Creator
        through endless nights and days.
     More eloquent than language,
        more radiant than the sun,
     this message of God's splendour
        is meant for everyone.

2   The law of God is perfect,
        its precepts always right,
     revealing timeless wisdom,
        providing life and light —
     no gold could be so precious,
        no honey taste as sweet;
     and those who yield obedience
        will find their joy complete.

3   Forgive my secret failures,
        the faults I do not know;
     from wilful sins protect me,
        and ways I should not go.
     May all my meditations,
        my every thought and word,
     be fashioned for your pleasure,
        my Saviour and my Lord.

MARTIN LECKEBUSCH (*b.* 1962)
based on Psalm 19

Music: GEORGE THALBEN-BALL (1896–1987)

YANWORTH   10 10 10 10

1   The Lord is King! He set the stars in space,
and fashioned all our varied human race.
Creator God whose hand sustains us still,
your kingdom stands, and all things serve your will.

2   The Lord is King! He sent his Son to earth,
his glory laid aside in human birth.
O Saviour Christ, who died and rose again,
your kingdom comes where in our lives you reign.

3   The Lord is King! He sent his Spirit here
to heal and save, to banish doubt and fear.
Spirit of truth, exalt the Living Word,
whose kingdom grows till all shall own him Lord.

4   The Lord is King! From all in earth and heaven
be blessing, honour, praise and glory given.
While earthly kingdoms fade and cease to be,
God's kingdom lasts for all eternity.

BRIAN HOARE (b. 1935)

Music: JOHN BARNARD (b. 1948)

1 The Lord's my shep-herd, I'll not want. He makes me lie in pas-tures green. He leads me by the still, still wa-ters, his good-ness re-stores my soul.

Refrain

Descant

I will trust, I will trust in you.

And I will trust in you a-lone, and I will

I will trust, I will trust in you. End-less mer-cy

trust in you a-lone, for your end-less mer-cy

fol-lows me, good-ness will lead me home.

fol-lows me, your good-ness will lead me home.

Music: STUART TOWNEND (*b.* 1963)

1 The Lord's my shepherd, I'll not want.
   He makes me lie in pastures green.
   He leads me by the still, still waters,
   his goodness restores my soul.

   And I will trust in you alone.
   And I will trust in you alone,
   for your endless mercy follows me,
   your goodness will lead me home.

   (Descant)
   I will trust, I will trust in you.
   I will trust, I will trust in you.
   Endless mercy follows me,
   goodness will lead me home.

2 He guides my ways in righteousness,
   and he anoints my head with oil,
   and my cup, it overflows with joy,
   I feast on his pure delights.

3 And though I walk the darkest path,
   I will not fear the evil one,
   for you are with me, and your rod and staff
   are the comfort I need to know.

   STUART TOWNEND (*b* 1963)
   based on Psalm 23

1 There is a Re - deem - er, Je - sus, God's own Son,_____
pre - cious Lamb of God, Mes - si - ah, Ho - - - - ly
One. *Thank you, O my Fa - - ther, for*
giv - ing us your Son,_____ and leav - - ing your
Spi - rit till the work__ on__ earth is done. done.

Music: MELODY GREEN
arranged by PETER MOGER (b. 1964)

1   There is a Redeemer,
Jesus, God's own Son,
precious Lamb of God, Messiah,
Holy One.

Thank you, O my Father,
for giving us your Son,
and leaving your Spirit
till the work on earth is done.

2   Jesus my Redeemer,
Name above all names,
precious Lamb of God, Messiah,
O for sinners slain:

3   When I stand in glory
I will see his face,
and there I'll serve my King for ever
in that holy place.

KEITH GREEN (1953–1982)
and MELODY GREEN

315 Words and Music: © 1982 Birdwing Music, BMG Songs Inc., Ears to Hear Music assigned to EMI Christian Music Publishing / Small Stone Media BV, Netherlands. Administered by Song Solutions CopyCare, 14 Horsted Square, Uckfield, East Sussex, TN22 1QG, United Kingdom. <info@songsolutions.org> Used by permission.

CORVEDALE   87 87 D

Descant *(v. 4)*

If our love were but more sim - - ple, we should

Unison

take him at his word;____ and our lives would be all

glad - ness in the joy of Christ____ our Lord.

Music: MAURICE BEVAN (1921–2006)

316   Music: © Cathedral Music, King Charles Cottage, Racton, Chichester, West Sussex. PO18 9DT

1   There's a wideness in God's mercy
      like the wideness of the sea;
    there's a kindness in his justice
      which is more than liberty.
    There is no place where earth's sorrows
      are more felt than up in heaven;
    there is no place where earth's failings
      have such kindly judgement given.

2   For the love of God is broader
      than the measure of our mind,
    and the heart of the Eternal
      is most wonderfully kind.
    But we make his love too narrow
      by false limits of our own;
    and we magnify his strictness
      with a zeal he would not own.

3   There is plentiful redemption
      through the blood that has been shed;
    there is joy for all the members
      in the sorrows of the Head.
    There is grace enough for thousands
      of new worlds as great as this;
    there is room for fresh creations
      in that upper home of bliss.

Second half of tune:

4   If our love were but more simple,
      we should take him at his word;
    and our lives would be all gladness
      in the joy of Christ our Lord.

* FREDERICK WILLIAM FABER (1814–1863)

HEANISH   87 87 D

1   We shall see him in the morning
        when the mists of life have cleared,
    with his arms outstretched to greet us
        from a journey we have feared.
    Those who toiled all night and struggled
        till the earthly fight was won
    will awaken to the music
        of his welcoming 'Well done!'

2   We shall recognize the Master
        with his wounded hands and side
    as we worship him, the glorious,
        the ascended Crucified.
    Though the shore now seems so distant
        we await the morning light
    and the breakfast celebration
        when our faith gives way to sight.

                                RANDLE MANWARING (b. 1912)

Music: JOHN BARNARD (b. 1948)

LUCERNA LAUDONIAE 77 77 77

1 Who can measure heaven and earth?
God was present at their birth;
who can number seeds or sands?
Every grain is in his hands:
   through creation's countless days
   every dawn sings out his praise.

2 Who can tell what Wisdom brings,
first of all created things?
One alone is truly wise,
hidden from our earthbound eyes:
   knowledge lies in him alone —
   God, the Lord upon his throne!

3 Wisdom in his plans he laid,
planted her in all he made;
granted her to humankind,
sowed her truth in every mind:
   but with richest wisdom blessed
   those who love him first and best.

4 Wisdom gives the surest wealth,
brings her children life and health;
teaches us to fear the Lord,
marks a universe restored:
   heaven and earth she will outlast —
   happy those who hold her fast!

CHRISTOPHER IDLE (*b.* 1938)
based on Ecclesiasticus 1

Music: DAVID EVANS (1874–1948)

EIFIONYDD   87 87 D

1   Year by year, from past to future
         worship marks our upward climb,
     sets the rhythm of our journey
         to eternity through time:
     though the outward things diminish
         we are held more firm by grace,
     following God's heavenward calling
         and the everlasting prize.

2   As we seek to weave life's fabric
         on the lengthening loom of days,
     may Christ guide the threads that form it,
         be the pattern it displays;
     may the Father, master craftsman,
         sorrowing over each mistake,
     plan for us a new perfection
         from the ugliness we make.

3   Though we long for the adventure
         of the mystery of bliss,
     to the pilgrim's eyes the pathway
         breaks, and ends in death's abyss;
     but within the dark are waiting
         hands that bear the print of nails,
     which will hold us safe and bear us
         where the worship never fails.

                                    ALAN LUFF (b. 1928)

Music: JOHN AMBROSE LLOYD (1815–1874)

Behold the Lamb of God,
behold the Lamb of God.
He takes away the sin,
the sin of the world.

JOHN L. BELL (b. 1949)
based on John 1.29

Music: JOHN L. BELL (b. 1949)

Come to me, come to me,
weak and heavy laden;
trust in me, lean on me.
I will give you rest.

JOHN L. BELL (b. 1949)
based on Matthew 11.28-29

Music: JOHN L. BELL (b. 1949)

Calm me, Lord, as you calmed the storm;
still me, Lord, keep me from harm.
Let all the tumult within me cease;
enfold me, Lord, in your peace.

DAVID ADAM (b. 1936)

Music: MARGARET RIZZA (b. 1929)

God is for-give-ness. Dare to for-give and God will be with you.

God is for-give--ness. Love, and do not fear.

God is forgiveness.
Dare to forgive and God will be with you.
God is forgiveness.
Love, and do not fear.

Taizé Community

Music: Taizé Community

Traditional

Music: Caribbean traditional
    arranged by GEOFF WEAVER (*b.* 1943)

(Last time)

(Last time)

In manus tuas, Pater,
commendo spiritum meum.
In manus tuas, Pater,
commendo spiritum meum.

*(Into your hands, Father,
I commend my spirit.)*

Taizé Community
based on Psalm 31.5, Luke 23.46

Music: Taizé Community

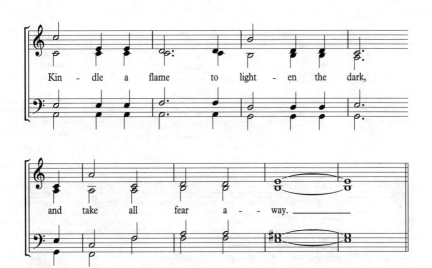

Kindle a flame to lighten the dark
and take all fear away.

JOHN L. BELL *(b. 1949)*
and GRAHAM MAULE *(b. 1958)*

Music: JOHN L. BELL *(b. 1949)*

326 Words and Music: From *Heaven Shall Not Wait*, 1987. © 1987, Wild Goose Resource Group, The Iona Community, 4th Floor, Savoy Centre, 140 Sauchiehall Street, Glasgow G2 3DH

Lord Je - sus Christ, your light shines with - in us. Let not my

doubts nor my dark - ness speak to me. Lord Je - sus Christ, your

light shines with - in us. Let my heart al - ways wel - come your love.

Some or all of the optional verses, for one or more cantors, may be added once the ostinato has been sung at least twice.

Music: JACQUES BERTHIER (1923–1994)

327 Words and Music: © 1998, Ateliers et Presses de Taizé, 71250 Taizé, France

Cantor(s)

1 Lord, you have searched me and known me; you know when I sit down, when I rise up. You are ac-quaint - ed with all my ways. 2 If I take the wings of the morn-ing, and set-tle at the farth - est li-mits of the sea, e-ven there your hand shall hold me fast. 3 If I say, 'Let the dark-ness co-ver me,' e-ven the dark ness-is not dark to you, and night is as bright as the day. 4 Search me, God, and know my heart and lead me in the ev - er-last-ing way.

1 2 3 4

* *Choose either part.*

Taizé Community
based on Psalm 139

Refrain

No - thing can ev - er come be - tween us and the love of God, the love of God re - vealed to us in Christ Je - - sus.

(Last time)

Verses

D.C.

The verses are sung by one or more voices (between repetitions of the refrain) while the accompanying chords are played or sung.

Music: Taizé Community

328 Words and Music: © 2007, Ateliers et Presses de Taizé, 71250 Taizé, France

GENERAL

Cantor(s)

1 When I am a-fraid, Lord, I put my trust in you. In you I trust; I shall not fear.

2 This I know, that God is on my side. In God I trust; I shall not fear.

3 I thank you, O Lord, you saved my soul from death, so I may walk in the light of the liv-ing.

4 If it is God who jus-ti-fies, who then may con-demn? The Fa-ther gave us his own Son.

5 It is Christ who died, Christ who rose a-gain. At the right hand of God, he prays for us.

6 Nei-ther death, nor life, nor things pre-sent or to come, no-thing can ev-er keep us from God's love.

Taizé Community
based on Psalm 56, Romans 8.31-39

O Lord, my heart is not proud, nor haugh-ty my
eyes.___ I have not gone__ af-ter things too great, nor
mar- - vels be- - yond me. Tru-ly I have set my
soul___ in si- -lence and peace;___ at

Music: MARGARET RIZZA (b. 1929)

O Lord, my heart is not proud,
  nor haughty my eyes.
I have not gone after things too great,
  nor marvels beyond me.
Truly I have set my soul in silence and peace;
at rest, as a child in its mother's arms,
  so is my soul.

from Psalm 131 in *The Grail Psalter*

Ostinato

With - in our dark - est night, you kin - dle the
fire that nev - er dies a - - way, that nev - er dies a - -
way. With - in our dark - est night, you kin - dle the
fire that nev - er dies a - - way, that nev - er dies a - - way.

(Last time)

Within our darkest night
you kindle the fire that never dies away,
    that never dies away.
Within our darkest night
you kindle the fire that never dies away,
    that never dies away.

Taizé Community

Music: JACQUES BERTHIER (1923–1994)

INDEXES

ALPHABETICAL INDEX OF TUNES

Tunes shown preceded by an asterisk are alternative names.

INDEX OF TUNES BY METRE

Alternative tune names are not shown in this index.

INDEX OF COMPOSERS, ARRANGERS and SOURCES of MUSIC

COMPOSER INDEX

INDEX OF AUTHORS
and SOURCES of WORDS

AUTHOR INDEX

INDEX OF FIRST LINES and TUNES

FIRST LINE INDEX